A–Z
of
MATHS
vocabulary

A teacher's survival guide for the primary curriculum

Full coverage of terminology
Simple definitions with examples

Paul Broadbent

Each entry is labelled with an icon which tells you its content domain:

1234 **Number and place value**

+−×÷ **Calculation**

½ 0.5 50% **Fractions, decimals and percentages**

▮▮ **Ratio and proportion**

x y z **Algebra**

📏 **Measurement**

○△□ **Geometry – properties of shape**

▦ **Geometry – position and direction**

|ıl.ıl **Statistics**

???? **Problem solving and general vocabulary**

Related words appear in red: ▶ sum, total

Published by Keen Kite Books
An imprint of HarperCollins*Publishers* Ltd
1 London Bridge Street
London SE1 9GF

ISBN 9780008192662

First published in 2016

10 9 8 7 6 5 4 3 2 1

Text © Paul Broadbent

Design © 2016 Keen Kite Books, an imprint of HarperCollins*Publishers* Ltd

Images: P7 © Gregory K. Scott/Science Photo Library; P15 GIPhotoStock/Science Photo Library.
All other images and illustrations are © Shutterstock.com & © HarperCollins*Publishers*

British Library Cataloguing in Publication Data.

A CIP record of this book is available from the British Library.

Commissioning Editor: Michelle I'Anson
Inside Concept Design: Paul Oates
Project Managers: Shelley Teasdale and Gwynneth Drabble
Cover Design: Anthony Godber
Text Design and Layout: Ian Wrigley
Production: Lyndsey Rogers
Printed by Martins The Printers, Berwick-upon-Tweed

Abacus (plural: abaci) KS1 1234

An abacus is a simple calculating tool. Stones, beads or rings are used to count and calculate. This example has beads that slide along rods.

In some countries abaci are still used to help calculate because they are quick to use. A **suan pan** is used in China and a **soroban** is used in Japan.

Acute angle KS2

An acute angle is smaller than a right-angle. It is an angle that is between 0° and 90°.

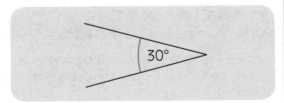

30°

▶ angle, obtuse angle, reflex angle, right angle

Addend KS1 +−×÷

An addend is a number that is added to another number.

7 + 5 = 12   7 and 5 are both addends, with the sum of 12.

▶ subtrahend

Addition (+) KS1 +−×÷

Addition is finding the total of two or more numbers. The + sign in a calculation shows that numbers are being added together.

The addition of 12 and 7 gives 19.

12 + 7 = 19

▶ sum, total

Adjacent KS2

Adjacent means near or next to something.

For this set of number cards, 4 is adjacent to 9.

▶ beside

Adjust KS2 ????

To adjust something means to change or alter it.

If you adjust the scale it will change the shape of a graph.

Algebra

KS2
xyz

Algebra is a branch of mathematics that uses letters or symbols to represent numbers and to make generalisations. It is used to help solve problems and investigate number patterns.

If $y + 3 = 5$, what is the value of y?

$y = 2$

▶ equation, formula

a.m.

KS2

The short way of writing 'ante meridiem' is a.m., which means before midday or noon.

The lessons started at 9.15 a.m.

▶ midday, p.m.

Analogue clock

KS1

An analogue clock measures time using hands moving around a dial.

▶ digital clock, time

Angle

KS1

The amount by which something turns is an angle. It is a measure of rotation, measured in degrees (°).

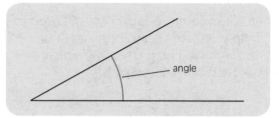

angle

▶ acute angle, degree, obtuse angle, reflex angle, right angle

Annual

KS2

An annual event is one that happens once a year.

Your birthday is an annual event. It would be great if you could celebrate it more than once a year!

Anticlockwise

KS1

When something turns anticlockwise, it goes round in the opposite direction to the hands on a clock.

▶ clockwise, rotate

Approximate
KS2 ????

An approximate answer is very close to the right answer, but not exact. The sign ≈ means 'is approximately equal to'.

> The approximate answer to 19 × 31 is 600.
>
> 19 × 31 ≈ 600

▶ estimate, round

Arc
KS2 ○△□

An arc is a curved line that would make a complete circle if you continued it. A rainbow is an arc of colour in the sky.

▶ chord, circle, circumference

Area
KS2

The area of a surface is a measure of how much space is covered by that surface. It is usually measured in square units such as square centimetres (cm^2) or square metres (m^2).

> The area of this rectangle is 12 squares.

▶ square centimetre

Arithmetic
KS1 +−×÷

Arithmetic is the branch of mathematics that involves handling numbers and calculating. It includes addition, subtraction, multiplication and division.

> Mental arithmetic is calculating in your head.

▶ addition, division, multiplication, subtraction

Array
KS1 1234

An array is a regular arrangement of numbers or objects. It has rows and columns, usually in the form of a rectangle.

> | 1 | 2 | 3 |
> |---|---|---|
> | 4 | 5 | 6 |
> | 7 | 8 | 9 |

Arrowhead
KS2 ○△□

An arrowhead is a quadrilateral with two pairs of equal sides and an angle greater than 180°. It is sometimes called a dart.

▶ quadrilateral, reflex angle

A B C D E F G H I J K L M N O P Q R S T U V W X Y Z

Ascending

Ascending means going up in order from smallest to largest.

> The numbers 3.2, 2.5, 2.3 and 5.2 written in ascending order are:
>
> 2.3, 2.5, 3.2, 5.2

▶ descending, order

Associative

Addition and multiplication are associative because the answer does not alter if pairs are grouped in different ways: $a + (b + c) = (a + b) + c$ and $a \times (b \times c) = (a \times b) \times c$
Subtraction and division are **not** associative.

> $9 + (3 + 5) = (9 + 3) + 5$
>
> $4 \times (2 \times 5) = (4 \times 2) \times 5$

▶ commutative, distributive

Average

The average of a group of numbers is a common (mode) or middle (median) value. The mean average of a set of numbers can be found by adding them and dividing the total by how many numbers there are.

> Hours of sunshine for five days
>
> | Mon | Tue | Wed | Thu | Fri |
> |-----|-----|-----|-----|-----|
> | 6 | 4 | 9 | 6 | 10 |
>
> Mode: 6 hours (two days with 6 hours)
> Median: 6 hours (4, 6, **6**, 9, 10)
> Mean: 7 hours
> $(6 + 4 + 9 + 6 + 10) \div 5 = 7$

▶ mean, median, mode

Average speed

The average speed is found by dividing the total distance travelled by the total journey time.

> A car travels 150 km in 2 hours. Its average speed is 75 km/h.

Axis (plural: axes)

An axis is the horizontal or vertical line on a graph. The axes are used to measure the position of points on the graph. The x-axis is the horizontal axis and the y-axis is the vertical axis.

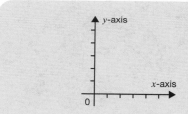

▶ coordinate

Axis of symmetry

An axis of symmetry is a line about which a shape can be reflected and stay the same shape.

> A rectangle has 2 axes of symmetry.
>
>

▶ line symmetry, rotational symmetry

Balance
KS1

A balance is another name for a weighing machine or scales. An object is put on one side and is balanced by weights on the other side.

Bar chart
KS1

A bar chart is a diagram used to represent statistical information using rows of horizontal or vertical bars. The bars have equal width and the length of each bar shows a certain amount. They are sometimes called bar graphs.

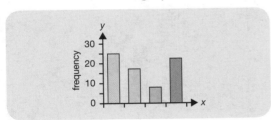

▶ bar-line graph

Bar-line graph
KS2

A bar-line graph is a bar chart where the bars are drawn as lines.

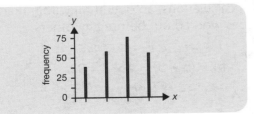

▶ bar chart

Base
KS1

The base of a shape or object is the bottom line or surface on which it rests.

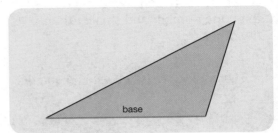

base

Bearing
KS2

A bearing gives the direction of a travelling object. It is the clockwise angle between the direction north and the direction being travelled. A bearing is always given as a 3-figure angle.

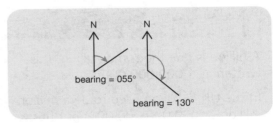

bearing = 055°

bearing = 130°

▶ angle, clockwise

Beside
KS1

To be beside something is to be close to it or next to it.

The triangle is beside the square.

▶ adjacent

A B C D E F G H I J K L M N O P Q R S T U V W X Y Z

Between   `KS1`

If something is between two other things it is in the space that separates them. A number between two others is bigger than one number and smaller than the other.

> The number 45 is between 44 and 46.

Beyond   `KS1`

To be beyond something is to be further than it or past it.

> If you choose a number beyond 10 000, it needs to be greater than 10 000.

Billion   `KS2` `1234`

A billion is one thousand million. It is written as 1 000 000 000.

In the UK, a billion used to be a million million (1 000 000 000 000) but this is no longer in common use.

> Saturn is just under 1.5 billion kilometres from the sun.

► giga-, million

Bisect   `KS2`

To bisect is to divide a line, angle or area exactly in half.

This 60° angle is bisected into two angles of 30°.

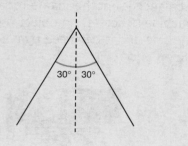

► divide, halve

Block graph   `KS1`

A block graph uses blocks to represent statistical data. Each block in a column or row represents one object or recording.

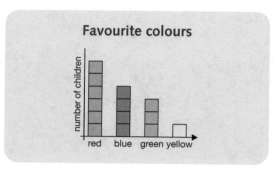

Favourite colours

► bar chart

Brackets   `KS2` `+−×÷`

Brackets are the symbols (,). Brackets are used to put items or numbers together. In calculations, an operation within brackets is worked out before any others.

> $4 \times (5 + 3) = 4 \times 8 = 32$
>
> $4 \times 5 + 3 = 20 + 3 = 23$

► calculate, operation

Breadth KS1

Breadth is another name for width. It is the distance across from one side to the other.

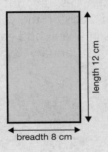

The breadth of this rectangle is 8 cm.

length 12 cm

breadth 8 cm

▶ length, width

British Summer Time (BST) KS2

British Summer Time (BST) is the period between March and October when clocks are put forward by 1 hour.

During British Summer Time clocks are changed to 7.00 a.m. when it is actually 6.00 a.m. for the rest of the year.

▶ Greenwich Mean Time

A
B
C
D
E
F
G
H
I
J
K
L
M
N
O
P
Q
R
S
T
U
V
W
X
Y
Z

C

C is the symbol which stands for 100 in the Roman number system.

> CX is 110.

▶ D, I, L, Roman numerals, V, X

Calculate

To calculate is to use numbers to work out an answer.

The word calculate comes from the Latin word *calculus* meaning a pebble used as a counter.

> Calculate the sum of the first five odd numbers.
>
> $1 + 3 + 5 + 7 + 9 = 25$

Calculator

A calculator is a pocket-sized computer, used for calculating.

Calendar

A calendar is a system for counting the years and dividing the years into months and days. Different calendars are used across the world.

The Gregorian calendar is used in most western countries. It counts years from the birth of Christ in the year AD 1, with 12 months in a year and each new year starting on 1st January.

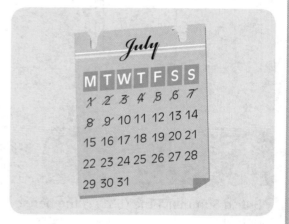

July

M	T	W	T	F	S	S
1	2	3	4	5	6	7
8	9	10	11	12	13	14
15	16	17	18	19	20	21
22	23	24	25	26	27	28
29	30	31				

▶ day, month, time, year

Cancel

To cancel is to simplify a fraction down to its lowest terms by dividing the numerator and denominator by the same number.

> You can cancel, or simplify, $\frac{12}{15}$ by dividing both numerator and denominator by 3.
>
> $\frac{12}{15} = \frac{4}{5}$

▶ denominator, lowest terms, numerator, reduce, simplify

Capacity

KS1

Capacity is the amount of space in a container or the amount of liquid it can hold.

This jug has a capacity of 5 litres.

▶ centilitre, gallon, litre, millilitre, pint, volume

Cardinal number

KS1
1234

Cardinal numbers are the counting numbers. They are numbers that show quantity but not order.

The cardinal numbers are 1, 2, 3, 4 ...

▶ ordinal number

Carroll diagram

KS1

A Carroll diagram is a grid used to sort things into groups or sets.

A mathematician called Charles Dodgson invented Carroll diagrams as an alternative to Venn diagrams. He is better known as Lewis Carroll, the author of *Alice's Adventures in Wonderland*.

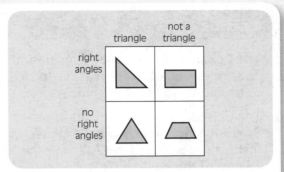

▶ set, sort, Venn diagram

Cartesian coordinates

KS2

Cartesian coordinates use two axes at right angles to each other to determine the position of a point. The horizontal axis is the x-axis and the vertical axis is the y-axis, with the ordered pair of numbers (x, y) defining the position of a point. The origin is the point $(0,0)$ at the intersection of the axes.

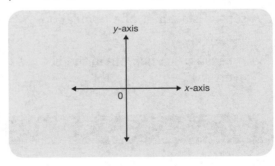

▶ axis, coordinate

Categorical data

KS1

Categorical data consists of discrete, unordered items, in two or more categories.

Collecting data about hair colour in a class is categorical data as there is no way of ordering it before the data is collected.

▶ data, discrete data

A B C D E F G H I J K L M N O P Q R S T U V W X Y Z

A B C D E F G H I J K L M N O P Q R S T U V W X Y Z

Celsius (°C) KS2

The Celsius scale measures temperature in degrees Celsius, written as °C. It used to be known as the centigrade scale.

The Celsius scale was named after a Swedish astronomer, Anders Celsius. His first scale, developed in 1742, was the reverse of the modern scale; he used 100 °C for the freezing point of water and 0 °C for the boiling point.

> On the Celsius scale, the freezing point of water is 0 °C and the boiling point of water is 100 °C.

▶ centigrade, Fahrenheit, temperature

Census KS2

A census is a count of a population.

> A census is carried out in the UK every 10 years.

Cent KS2 1234

A cent is a unit of money used in some countries. Its value is $\frac{1}{100}$ of the main currency unit.

> There are 100 cents in one Euro.

Centi- KS1

Centi- is a prefix meaning $\frac{1}{100}$. If it is written before a word it usually means divided into hundredths, or one-hundredth.

> A centimetre is $\frac{1}{100}$ of 1 metre.

▶ giga-, kilo-, mega-, milli-

Centigrade KS2

The centigrade scale is used for measuring temperature. Centigrade is now usually replaced by Celsius as it uses the same scale.

> On a hot day the temperature can reach 30 °C, which is 30° centigrade or 30° Celsius.

▶ Celsius, Fahrenheit, temperature

Centilitre (cl) KS2

A centilitre is a measure of capacity in the metric system. It is equal to $\frac{1}{100}$ litre.

> There are 10 ml in 1 cl.

▶ litre, metric unit

Centimetre (cm)
KS1

A centimetre is a measure of length in the metric system. It is equal to $\frac{1}{100}$ metre.

> The width of your little finger is about 1 cm.

1 cm

▶ metre, metric system, millimetre

Centre
KS1

The centre is the middle point of a shape or object. The centre of a circle is exactly the same distance from every place on its circumference.

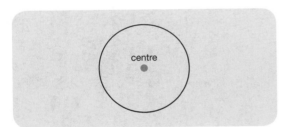

centre

▶ circle, circumference, diameter

Centre of rotation
KS2

The centre of rotation is the point around which a shape can turn or rotate.

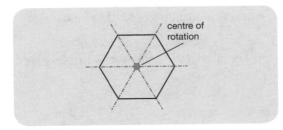

centre of rotation

▶ rotate, rotational symmetry

Century
KS1

A period of 100 years is called a century.

> We are now in the 21st century.

▶ decade, millennium, year

Change
KS1

Change is the amount of money you are given back if you pay more than the price of an item.

> If a T-shirt costs £4.60 and I pay £5 I will get 40p change.

Chord
KS2

A chord is a straight line that joins the ends of an arc of a circle.

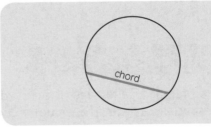

chord

▶ arc, circle, circumference, diameter

Chronological
KS1

When items are arranged in order of time, starting with the earliest, they are in chronological order.

> These years are in chronological order: 1574, 1589, 1635, 1780, 1854.

A B C D E F G H I J K L M N O P Q R S T U V W X Y Z

Circle

A circle is a shape with every point at its edge at exactly the same distance from the centre.

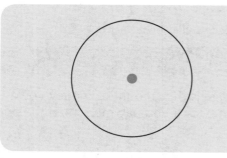

▶ centre, circumference, diameter, radius

Circular

A shape or object that is in the form of a circle.

> A full moon is circular in shape.

▶ circle

Circumference

The circumference is the edge of a curved shape, especially a circle. The circumference is also the length of that edge.

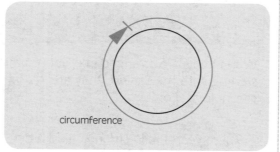

circumference

▶ circle, diameter, perimeter, pi, radius

Classify

To classify data or information is to arrange it into groups or classes.

> To interpret data on traffic going past the school, we could classify it into types of vehicle.

▶ data

Clear

The 'clear' key on a calculator clears the display ready for a new calculation. If there is something in the memory this will still be stored until the calculator is switched off or the MC key pressed.

clear

Climate

The climate of a place is the average weather conditions of that place.

> The climate in Western Europe is wet and mild.

▶ temperature

Clinometer • Common factor

Clinometer

KS2

A clinometer is a hand-held instrument for measuring the angle of elevation (or depression) of something. It is used to work out the heights of objects such as trees and buildings.

Clockwise

KS1

When something turns clockwise, it goes round in the same direction as the hands on a clock.

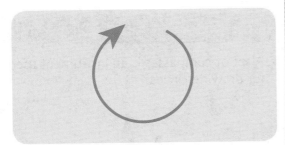

▶ anticlockwise, rotate

Column

KS2 1234

A column is a vertical arrangement going up or down.

1	2	3	4
5	6	7	8
9	10	11	12

The numbers in the first column are 1, 5 and 9.

▶ row

Column graph

KS1

A bar chart with bars that are arranged vertically.

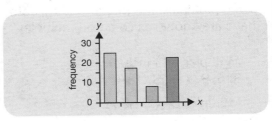

▶ bar chart

Common factor

KS2 1234

A factor is a whole number that divides exactly into another number. A common factor is a number which is a factor of two or more numbers.

These are the factors of 12 and 18:

12: **1, 2, 3**, 4, **6**, 12

18: **1, 2, 3, 6**, 9, 18

The common factors are 1, 2, 3 and 6.

▶ factor, highest common factor

A B C D E F G H I J K L M N O P Q R S T U V W X Y Z

Common fraction

KS1

A common fraction (also known as a simple fraction or a vulgar fraction) is a fraction written in the form of two numbers, one above the other, separated by a line. The bottom number (denominator) cannot be a 1 or zero. The line shows a division, with the upper number (numerator) to be divided by the denominator.

$\frac{3}{5}$, $\frac{7}{10}$ and $\frac{19}{50}$ are all common fractions.

▶ denominator, fraction, numerator

Common multiple

KS2

If two or more numbers have some of the same multiples, the multiples they both have are known as common multiples.

Multiples of 3 include:
3, 6, 9, 12, 15, 18, 21, 24

Multiples of 4 include:
4, 8, 12, 16, 20, 24, 28

Common multiples of 3 and 4 include 12 and 24

▶ multiple

Commutative

KS1

An operation is commutative if the order of operating does not matter. Addition and multiplication are commutative operations because $a + b = b + a$ and $a \times b = b \times a$. Subtraction and division are not commutative.

$$8 + 5 = 5 + 8 \qquad 3 \times 6 = 6 \times 3$$

▶ associative, distributive

Compare

KS1

When you compare two objects or numbers you look for differences and similarities between them.

When you compare a square and a rhombus, you see that they both have four equal sides, but the square has right angles.

Compass

KS1

A compass is an instrument used to find the direction of north. It has a magnetic needle that always points to north. Once north is found, other directions can then be read on the compass.

▶ bearing

Compasses

KS2

A set of compasses is an instrument used for drawing circles.

▶ circle

Compensation

KS1 +−×÷

We use compensation after using rounding to make calculations easier. The calculation is then adjusted by compensating the added or subtracted amount.

> 74 + 48
>
> Round 48 to 50: 74 + 50 = 124
>
> Subtract 2 to compensate:
> 124 − 2 = 122

▶ adjust, calculate, rounding

Complement

KS1 +−×÷

A number and its complement make a total.

> To make a total of 100, the number 45 has a complement of 55.

▶ partition, total

Composite shape

KS2 ○△□

A composite shape is a shape made by combining two or more shapes. It is sometimes called a compound shape. To work out the area of composite shapes it is often easier to split them into simpler shapes like rectangles.

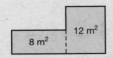

The area of this composite shape is 20 m².

▶ area, shape

Concave

KS2 ○△□

A concave surface curves inwards, like the inside of a spoon.

concave

▶ convex, shape

Concentric

KS2 ○△□

Two or more curved shapes are concentric if they have the same centre point.

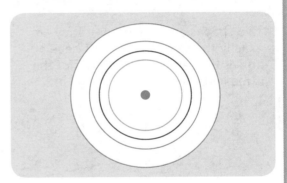

▶ circle

Concrete objects

KS1 ????

Items that can be handled and manipulated to help understand particular concepts and ideas.

> Abaci, base 10 apparatus, cuisenaire rods and shape tiles are all concrete objects.

▶ abacus

A B C D E F G H I J K L M N O P Q R S T U V W X Y Z

Cone
KS1

A cone is a three-dimensional shape with a circular base and a vertex commonly above the centre of the base. Line segments join all the points of the circle to the vertex forming a curved surface.

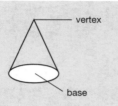

vertex

base

▶ base, solid figure, three-dimensional shape, vertex

Congruent
KS2

Two shapes are congruent if they are exactly the same. They must have all angles the same size and sides of the same lengths.

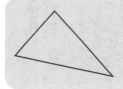 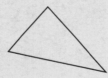

▶ angle, similar figure

Conjecture
KS1
????

A conjecture is a statement which may have evidence to support it, but has not yet been proved to be true or false.

> I am making a conjecture that the 10th number in this sequence will be 89.
> 1, 1, 2, 3, 5, 8…

Consecutive
KS1
1234

Consecutive means one after the other in order.

> 2, 4, 6, 8, 10… are consecutive even numbers.

Constant
KS2
+−×÷

A constant is a value that is unchanged when it is used.

> $a = 2b + 4$
> In this equation, the 2 and 4 are constants, and a and b are variables.

▶ equation, variable

Continuous data
KS1

Continuous data is data from measurements which may be arranged in groups with no gaps. It is often shown using a line graph.

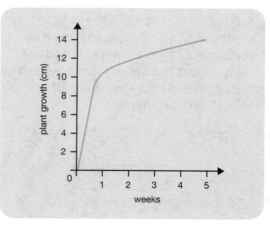

▶ data, discrete data, line graph

Convert
KS2
????

To convert something is to change it from one form to another. A conversion chart or graph can help work out the conversion.

> To convert centimetres to inches, multiply by 0.3937.
>
> 1 cm = 0.3937 inches

▶ exchange rate

Convex
KS2
○△□

A convex surface curves outwards, like the outside of a spoon.

convex

▶ concave

Coordinate
KS2

Coordinates are numbers that give the position of a point on a graph or grid. The numbers are usually written as a pair. The first coordinate gives the distance along the horizontal axis; the second coordinate gives the distance along the vertical axis.

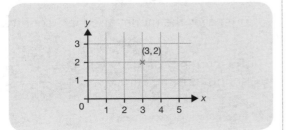

▶ axis, cartesian coordinates, grid, x-axis, y-axis

Corner
KS1
○△□

A corner is a point where two or more lines meet.

> A square has four corners.

▶ vertex

Correspondence problems
KS2
+−×÷

Correspondence problems involve the possible number of combinations of different objects.

> Ice-creams are sold in 3 sizes and 4 flavours. How many different types of ice-cream are there?

Count
KS1
1234

When you count you say (in your head or aloud) numbers in a certain order. When you count objects you find out how many there are by matching each object with a number name.

There are 1, 2, 3, 4, 5, **6** spots.

A B C D E F G H I J K L M N O P Q R S T U V W X Y Z

A B C D E F G H I J K L M N O P Q R S T U V W X Y Z

Cross-section `KS2`

A cross-section of a three-dimensional shape is a slice through it at right angles to one of its dimensions, such as its length or its height.

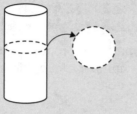

The cross-section of this cylinder is a circle.

▶ dimensions, polyhedron, three-dimensional

Cube `KS1`

A cube is a three-dimensional shape with six identical square faces.

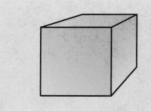

▶ cuboid, polyhedron, square, three-dimensional

Cube number `KS2` `1234`

A cube number is the product of three equal numbers. To show a number is cubed, a small number 3 is written using index notation.

$$4^3 = 4 \times 4 \times 4 = 64$$

▶ index, product

Cubic centimetre (cm³) `KS2`

A unit of volume, 1 cm³ is equivalent to the space taken by a cube with edges of 1 cm in length.

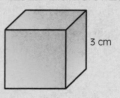

This cube has a volume of 27 cm³.

3 cm

▶ volume

Cuboid `KS1`

A cuboid is a three-dimensional shape with six rectangular faces.

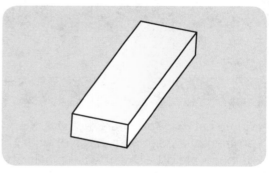

▶ cube, polyhedron, rectangle, three-dimensional

Currency `KS2` `????`

Currency is the money used in a country.

The currency of many European countries is the Euro.

▶ denomination, exchange rate

Curve

KS1

A curve is a line that is not straight.

Curved surface

KS2

A curved surface is any surface on a three-dimensional shape that is not flat.

Cones, cylinders and spheres each have curved surfaces.

► cone, cylinder, sphere

Cylinder

KS1

A cylinder is a three-dimensional shape with circles the same size at each end. It has the same circular cross-section all along its length. If a shape is cylindrical it is shaped like a cylinder.

► circle, cross-section

D KS2 1234

D is the symbol which stands for 500 in the Roman number system.

$$D + D = M$$

▶ C, I, L, M, Roman numerals, V, X

Daily KS1

Something done daily is done on every day of the week.

Many newspapers are produced daily.

▶ day

Dart

▶ arrowhead

Data KS1

Data is a set of numbers or information that can be collected, measured or recorded.

Lists of names and addresses are examples of data.

Database KS1

A database is a large amount of information stored in an organised way, often on a computer.

A database can be set up to store names and addresses.

▶ computer

Day KS1

A day lasts for 24 hours, starting at midnight.

24 hours is the length of time that the Earth takes to make one complete turn on its axis. The sun rises and sets once during a day.

There are seven days in a week.

▶ daily, hour, week, month, time, year

Deca- KS2 1234

Deca- is a prefix meaning 10.

A decagon is a polygon with 10 sides.

▶ centi-, kilo-, giga-, mega-, milli-, polygon

Decade KS2

A decade is a time period of ten years.

The 2000s was the decade from 1st January 2000 to 31st December 2009.

▶ century, time, year

Decagon KS2

A decagon is a 10-sided polygon.

This is a regular decagon.

▶ polygon

Decahedron
KS2

A decahedron is a polyhedron with 10 faces.

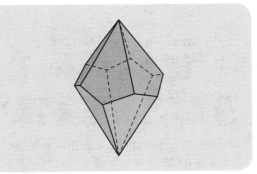

▶ polyhedron, three-dimensional

Decimal fraction
KS2

The part of a decimal number to the right of the decimal point is called the decimal fraction. It is a number less than 1.

0.85 is $\frac{8}{10} + \frac{5}{100} = \frac{85}{100}$

Decimal number
KS2

A decimal number is any number made up of the digits 0 to 9 using the base 10 number system.

127.6 is $100 + 20 + 7 + \frac{6}{10}$

Decimal place
KS2

The position of a digit after the decimal point is known as its decimal place.

1.845 has 3 decimal places.

Decimal point
KS2

A decimal point is used to show which digits are whole numbers and which are fractions. The digits to the left of the decimal point give the number of ones, tens, hundreds and thousands. The digits to the right of the decimal point give the number of tenths, hundredths, thousandths and so on.

Decimal points vary around the world. In France, for example, a comma is used instead of a decimal point.

1632.951

The digits 1, 6, 3 and 2 represent the whole number and the digits 9, 5 and 1 represent the fraction.

▶ digit, fraction, whole number

Decrease
KS1

If you decrease something you make it less or reduce it.

If you decrease a number by 20 you take 20 away from it.

▶ increase

Define
KS1

You define something by explaining it, giving its precise meaning.

You define a quadrilateral by describing its properties.

A B C D E F G H I J K L M N O P Q R S T U V W X Y Z

Degree (°) KS2

1. A degree is a unit of measure of temperature.

> Water boils at 100 degrees Celsius (100 °C).

▶ Celsius, temperature

2. A degree is also a unit of measure of angles.

> A complete circle is divided into 360 degrees (360°).

▶ angle

Denomination KS1

The value of coins and notes in the currency of a country.

> The 1p coin is the smallest denomination of currency in the UK.

▶ currency

Denominator KS2

The denominator is the number below the line in a fraction. It shows how many parts a whole shape or number of items is divided into.

> In the fraction $\frac{1}{4}$, the denominator is 4. $\frac{1}{4}$ of 12 is $12 \div 4 = 3$

▶ fraction, numerator

Depth KS1

When something is at a certain depth, it is that distance under the ground or below sea level.

> The shipwreck was found at a depth of 40 metres.

Descending KS1 1234

Descending means going down in order from largest to smallest.

> The numbers 47, 58, 39 and 61 written in descending order are:
> 61, 58, 47, 39

▶ ascending, order

Diagonal KS2

A diagonal line joins together two corners inside a shape such as a rectangle. The corners joined by a diagonal are not adjacent to each other.

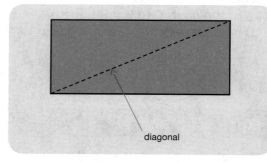

diagonal

▶ adjacent

Diameter
KS2

The diameter is a line that passes from one side of a circle or sphere through the centre to the other side. The diameter cuts a circle in half.

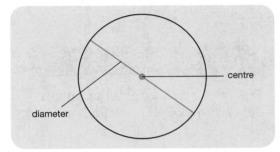

centre

diameter

► circle, radius, semicircle, sphere

Diamond

► rhombus

Die (plural: dice)
KS1
????

A die is usually a cube, with a number from 1 to 6 marked on each face. On a 1–6 die the numbers on opposite faces always add up to seven.

Difference
KS1
+−×÷

The difference is the amount by which one number or value is greater than another. You can also work out the difference between two numbers by subtracting the smaller one from the larger one.

The difference between 17 and 25 is 8.

25 − 17 = 8

► subtraction

Digit
KS1
1234

A digit is any of the ten numerals: 0, 1, 2, 3, 4, 5, 6, 7, 8 or 9. Numbers are made up of digits. The position of a digit in a number gives its value.

The number 847 has three digits.

► numeral

Digital clock
KS1

A digital clock shows the time using digits rather than by having hands on a dial.

► analogue clock, time

Dimensions

The dimensions of an object or shape are its sizes in different directions.

A flat shape has 2 dimensions because it has length and width but no height. A solid shape has 3 dimensions: length, width and height.

The dimensions of this box are 15 cm long, 12 cm wide and 8 cm high.

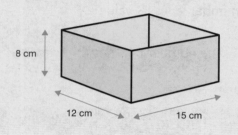

8 cm

12 cm   15 cm

▶ three-dimensional, two-dimensional

Disc

KS2

A disc is a flat circular shape.

Discount

KS2

A discount is an amount subtracted from the original price of an item.

The £48 coat has a discount of 50%, so it now costs £24.

Discrete data

KS2

Separate or distinct groups or items of data are known as discrete data.

Shoe sizes are discrete data.

▶ categorical data, continuous data, data

Distance

KS1

Distance is the length between two points.

The distance between the two villages is 17 km.

▶ length

Distribution

KS2

A distribution is a collection of measurements or data, distributed between the minimum and maximum values.

This chart shows the distribution of shoe sizes for a group of people:

shoe size	2	3	4	5	6
number of people	8	11	17	14	9

Distributive
KS2 +−×÷

An operation is distributive over another operation if the operations can be linked together in a certain way. Multiplication is distributive over addition and subtraction because $a(b + c) = ab + ac$. Division is distributive over addition because $\frac{a + b}{c} = \frac{a}{c} + \frac{b}{c}$

> $25 \times 3 = \underline{\quad}$
>
> $3(20 + 5) = (3 \times 20) + (3 \times 5)$

▶ associative, commutative, operation

Divide
KS1 +−×÷

To divide means to carry out the operation of division; sharing or grouping a quantity into a number of equal parts.

> When you divide 15 by 3 the answer is 5.

▶ division

Dividend
KS1 +−×÷

When carrying out the operation of division, the dividend is the number that is being divided.

> $24 \div 4 = 6$
>
> The dividend is 24, the divisor is 4 and the quotient is 6.

▶ numerator, division, divisor, quotient

Divisible
KS2 +−×÷

A whole number is divisible by another if it can be divided exactly by that number leaving no remainder.

> 42, 81 and 105 are all divisible by 3.

Division (÷)
KS1 +−×÷

Division is an operation on numbers in which a number is shared or grouped equally into a number of parts. The answer is called the quotient.

> Division is the inverse or opposite of multiplication.

▶ divide, dividend, multiplication, operation, quotient

Divisor
KS2 +−×÷

A divisor is a number that another number is divided by.

> For $27 \div 3$, the divisor is 3.

▶ denominator, dividend, quotient

Dodecagon
KS2 ○△□

A dodecagon is a 12-sided polygon.

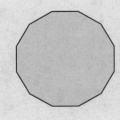

This is a regular dodecagon.

▶ polygon

A B C D E F G H I J K L M N O P Q R S T U V W X Y Z

Dodecahedron

 KS2

A dodecahedron is a 12-faced polyhedron. The faces of a regular dodecahedron are regular pentagons. A dodecahedron has 30 edges and 20 vertices.

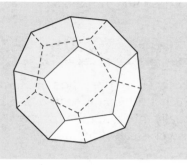

▶face, edge, pentagon, polyhedron, vertex

Double

KS1
+−×÷

1. To double is to multiply by 2.

   If you double 15 the answer is 30.

2. The number that is twice another number is a double.

   The double of 4 is 8.

Dozen

KS1
1234

A dozen is a group of 12.

This box holds one dozen eggs.

East KS1

East is one of the four main points of the compass, opposite to west and 90° clockwise from north.

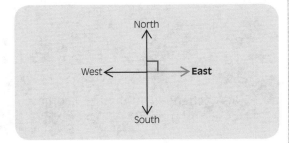

▶ compass, north, south, west

Edge KS1

The edge of a three-dimensional shape is where two or more faces meet. The edge of a two-dimensional shape is usually called a side.

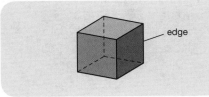

▶ face, side, vertex

Ellipse KS2

An ellipse is a special oval shape. It is like a squashed circle, with two lines of symmetry.

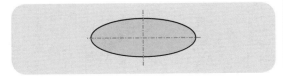

▶ circle, oval

Equal (=) KS1

If one amount equals another then they have the same value. The symbol = is read as 'is equal to' or 'equals'.

150 pence equals £1.50.

▶ inequality

Equation KS2

An equation is a statement showing that things are equal. Every equation has an equals sign which shows that the numbers on either side of it are the same, or equal.

$y = 8 - 2$

In this equation, $y = 6$.

▶ algebra, equal, formula

Equilateral triangle KS2

All three sides of an equilateral triangle are the same length. Each of the angles are also equal, at 60°.

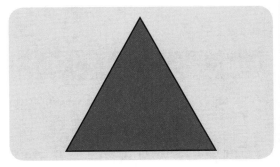

▶ polygon, isosceles triangle, right-angled triangle, scalene triangle

A B C D E F G H I J K L M N O P Q R S T U V W X Y Z

A
B
C
D
E
F
G
H
I
J
K
L
M
N
O
P
Q
R
S
T
U
V
W
X
Y
Z

Equivalent fraction
KS1
$\frac{1}{2}$ 0.5 50%

An equivalent fraction is a fraction with the same value as another.

These are all equivalent fractions:

$\frac{1}{2} = \frac{2}{4} = \frac{3}{6} = \frac{4}{8}$

▶ fraction

Estimate
KS1
+−×÷

To estimate a number means to decide roughly how big that number is.

I estimate that there are 200 words on this page.

▶ approximate, compensation

Even number
KS1
1234

An even number can be divided by 2 without leaving a remainder.

All even numbers end with the digits 0, 2, 4, 6 or 8. So 1356 is an even number.

▶ odd number

Exact
KS1
+−×÷

An exact number is the true value, **not** an approximate answer.

The exact answer to 38 × 17 is 646.

▶ approximate, compensation

Exchange
KS2
+−×÷

When a number is changed for another of equal value, often during a written calculation, it uses the process of exchange.

$$\begin{array}{r} {}^{7}\cancel{8}{}^{1}4 \\ -38 \\ \hline 46 \end{array}$$

10 is exchanged so that it becomes 14 − 8 and then 70 − 30.

Exchange rate
KS2
????

The exchange rate is the rate at which the currency of one country is exchanged for that of another.

The exchange rate for £ (pounds sterling) to $ (US dollars) is approximately £1 = $1.60.

▶ convert, currency

Face

A flat surface of a polyhedron is called a face.

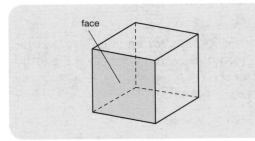

face

▶ edge, polyhedron, vertex

Factor

KS2 1234

A factor is a whole number that divides exactly into another number without leaving a remainder.

> 4 is a factor of 12 as it divides exactly into 12. 12 has six factors: 1, 2, 3, 4, 6 and 12.

Factorise

KS2 1234

To factorise is to break up or separate a number into the product of its factors. This can be useful for mental calculations.

> 24 may be factorised into:
>
> 2 × 3 × 4
>
> or
>
> 4 × 6
>
> or
>
> 3 × 8

Fahrenheit (°F)

Fahrenheit refers to the Fahrenheit scale used for measuring temperature.

This temperature scale is named after G.D. Fahrenheit, a German physicist from the beginning of the 18th century. The boiling point of water on the Fahrenheit scale is 212 °F and the freezing point is 32 °F.

> On a warm day the temperature can reach 70 °F.

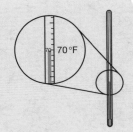

70° 70 °F

▶ Celsius, centigrade, temperature

Fibonacci sequence

KS2 1234

A Fibonacci sequence is one where each number is found by adding the two previous numbers. The first two numbers are 1, 1…

Leonardo Fibonacci was a 13th century Italian mathematician.

> 1, 1, 2, 3, 5, 8, 13, 21… is a Fibonacci sequence.

▶ sequence

First (1st)

KS1 1234

The first is the earliest in an order.

> The first even number is 2.

Flow chart • Fraction

Flow chart KS1

A flow chart is a diagram that shows the steps you must follow to solve a problem.

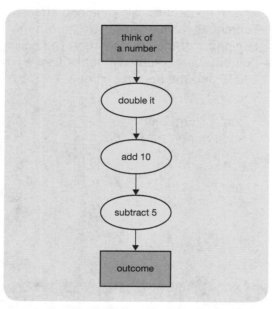

Foot (ft) KS2

A foot is an imperial unit of length equal to 12 inches.

The Ancient Greeks and the Romans were the first to use standard units. The Romans made copper bars one foot long and divided into twelve equal parts as a standard unit, which probably matched the length of an emperor's foot. The feet and inches used in modern times are based on the Roman foot.

> Most doors are about 6 and a half feet in height, which is approximately 2 metres.

▶ imperial system, inch, metre, mile, yard

Formula (plural: formulae) KS2

A formula is a rule that tells you how to work out something when you are given certain values.

> The formula for finding the area of a rectangle is area = length × breadth or $a = l \times b$.

▶ algebra, equation

Fortnight KS1

A fortnight is two weeks or 14 days.

> The home matches of my football team are every fortnight.

▶ day, week

Fraction KS1

A fraction is a number that is part of a whole number which results from dividing one integer by a second integer. Fractions can be written in different ways. A vulgar or common fraction is written with a numerator and denominator, such as $\frac{3}{4}$, and a decimal fraction is written as a decimal, such as 0.75.

> $\frac{2}{3}$, $1\frac{1}{4}$, $3\frac{1}{5}$ and 3.25 are all fractions.

▶ decimal fraction, improper fraction, mixed number, proper fraction

Frequency

The number of times that something happens is called the frequency.

The frequency of trains stopping at the station is three every hour.

Frequency table

A frequency table or chart is a way of recording information. It shows the number of times something happens.

Car colours	Frequency
red	50
white	36
blue	53

This shows the number of different colour cars passing the school in one hour.

Function

A function is a rule for changing one set of numbers into another, keeping the same relationship between input and output numbers. Function machines can be drawn to show functions.

The function for this change is ×2 + 1:

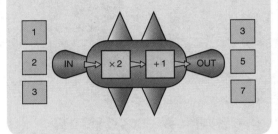

▶ relationship

Gallon

A gallon is an imperial unit of capacity. It measures the amount, or volume, of liquids. There are 8 pints in 1 gallon.

> A bucket holds approximately two gallons.

▶ imperial system, pint

General statement

When a general rule or statement is formulated then you are generalising or making a generalisation. A general statement is a statement that applies to all cases rather than just individual cases.

> The angle sum of triangles is 180°. This is a general statement that can be proved.

Geometry

Geometry is the part of mathematics that studies shapes, lines and angles. Geometrical shapes are made from straight lines and parts of circles.

> A geometry set includes a ruler, set-square, compasses and protractor for drawing shapes.

Giga-

Giga- is a prefix meaning 1 000 000 000, or 1 billion.

> A memory stick can have 1 gigabyte of memory.

▶ billion, centi-, deca-, kilo-, mega-, milli-

Gram (g)

A gram is a unit of mass or weight in the metric system. It is a very small mass – there are 1000 grams in 1 kilogram.

> A paper clip has a mass of about 1 g.

▶ kilogram, mass, metric system

Graph

A graph is a diagram that shows how one thing relates to another. Graphs often have a horizontal axis and a vertical axis.

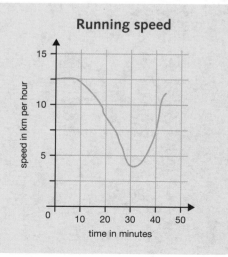

▶ axis, bar chart, coordinate

Greater than (>)

KS1 1234

If one quantity is more than a second quantity then it is greater than that second quantity.

$$\frac{2}{3} > \frac{1}{2}$$

This shows that $\frac{2}{3}$ is greater than $\frac{1}{2}$.

▶ less than, more than

Greenwich Mean Time

KS2

This is the local time for places on the same line as the Meridian of Greenwich, London.

In the UK we use Greenwich Mean Time as our actual time, with other countries equal to, more or less than this time.

▶ British Summer Time

Grid

KS2

A grid on a map or plan is a set of numbered or lettered squares. Using a grid helps us to find exact places by using coordinates.

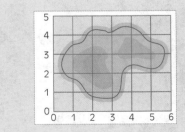

▶ coordinates

A B C D E F G H I J K L M N O P Q R S T U V W X Y Z

Half (plural: halves)
KS1 ½ 0.5 50%

A half is a fraction written as $\frac{1}{2}$. When something is divided into two equal parts, each part is one half.

> $\frac{1}{2}$ of 16 is 8.

► fraction

Halve
KS1 + − × ÷

To halve something is to divide it into two equal parts.

> If you halve a rectangle you can form two right-angled triangles.

► bisect, divide

Hectare
KS2

A hectare is a metric measure of area. 1 hectare = 10 000 square metres.

> A square with sides of 100 metres covers an area of 1 hectare.

► area, metric system, square metre

Height
KS1

The height of something is how tall it is.

> The height of a door is about 2 metres.

Hemisphere
KS2 ○ △ □

A hemisphere is half a sphere, made by cutting through the centre of a sphere.

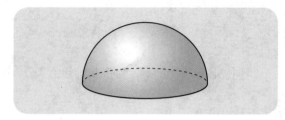

► sphere

Heptagon
KS2 ○ △ □

A heptagon is a polygon with seven straight sides.

This is a regular heptagon.

► polygon

Hexagon
KS2 ○ △ □

A hexagon is a polygon with six straight sides.

This is a regular hexagon.

► polygon

Highest common factor (HCF)

KS2 1234

The highest common factor (HCF) is the greatest whole number that divides exactly into two or more other numbers.

> The common factors of 16 and 24 are 1, 2, 4 and 8, so the highest common factor is 8.

► common factor, factor

Horizontal

KS2

1. Horizontal means in the same direction as the horizon, which is the distant line where the land and sky seem to meet.

KS2

2. A horizontal line is a straight, level line going across, perpendicular to the vertical.

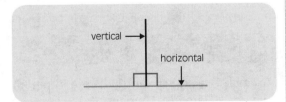

vertical
horizontal

► perpendicular, vertical

Hour

KS1

An hour is a measurement of time, lasting 60 minutes. There are 24 hours in a day.

> There is one hour between these two times.

► day, hour, minute, second, time

Hundredth

KS2 1234

1. Hundredth (100th) is the ordinal number of a hundred.

> On its hundredth throw the coin turned up heads.

KS2 $\frac{1}{2}$ 0.5 50%

2. A hundredth is the fraction $\frac{1}{100}$.

> A penny is a hundredth of a pound.

I

KS2 1234

I is the symbol which stands for 1 in the Roman number system.

> III stands for 3.

► C, D, L, M, Roman numerals V, X

Icosahedron

KS2

An icosahedron is a 20-faced polyhedron. All the faces of a regular icosahedron are equilateral triangles.

► polyhedron

Identical

KS2

If two shapes, measures or numbers are exactly the same, they are identical.

> These triangles are identical.

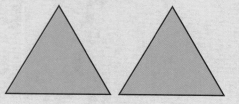

Imperial system

KS2

The imperial system is a set of measuring units which was once used throughout the UK. The system includes measures of length, such as yards, feet and inches; measures of weight, such as pounds and ounces; and measures of capacity, such as gallons and pints.

> A yard is 3 feet and is approximately 1 metre in length.

► foot, gallon, inch, metric system, ounce, pint, pound, yard

Improper fraction

KS2 ½ 0.5 50%

An improper fraction is a fraction that has a numerator greater than the denominator. Its value is greater than 1.

> $\frac{9}{4}$ is an improper fraction and is the same as the mixed number $2\frac{1}{4}$.

► denominator, fraction, mixed number, numerator

Inch

KS2

An inch is a unit of length in the imperial system. There are 12 inches in 1 foot. 1 inch is approximately 2.54 cm.

The inch was originally defined by Edward II. It was the length of three barley grains end to end.

> 1 inch

► foot, imperial system, mile, yard

Increase

KS1 +−×÷

If you increase something you make it more or larger.

> If you increase a number by 15 you add 15 to it.

▶ decrease

Index (plural: indices)

KS2 1234

Index notation is used when indices are written as a small digit at the top right of a number. It tells you the number of times the number is multiplied by itself. The index can also be called the power.

> $4^3 = 4 \times 4 \times 4 = 64$. The index is 3.

▶ cube number, square number

Inequality

KS1 1234

When one number or quantity is not equal to another.

> $3 + 5 > 6$ $7 + 4 < 20 − 5$

▶ equal

Infinity (∞)

KS2 1234

Infinity is a quantity larger than any known quantity.

> If you count for ever there will always be a bigger number than the last one you counted, so infinity is never-ending.

Integer

KS2 1234

An integer is another name for a whole number. It includes positive and negative numbers. Zero is also an integer.

> −5, −3, 0, 4 and 7 are all integers.

▶ negative number, positive number, whole number

Interpret

KS2

To interpret is to explain and describe something.

> You interpret a graph by looking at it and describing the results that it shows.

Interrogate

KS2

To interrogate a database is to explore its contents.

> You need to interrogate a database on birds to find out different wing-spans.

Intersection

KS2

An intersection is a crossing point or place. Two lines intersect at a point.

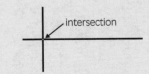

intersection

A B C D E F G H I J K L M N O P Q R S T U V W X Y Z

Interval

An interval is a period of time. It can also mean the difference between two numbers.

> There is an interval of 5 between the numbers 4 and 9.

▶ difference

Inverse

The inverse is the reverse or opposite of something.

> Addition is the inverse of subtraction.

Irregular

Irregular objects do not follow a given pattern or format.

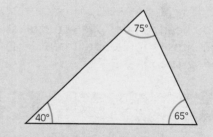

> This scalene triangle is irregular because it has three different angles and sides of different lengths.

▶ regular, scalene triangle

Isosceles triangle

An isosceles triangle has two equal sides with the opposite angles also equal.

The word isosceles comes from two Greek words, *isos* meaning equal and *skelos* meaning leg.

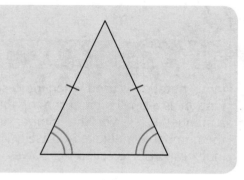

▶ equilateral triangle, right-angled triangle, scalene triangle

Justify

When you justify a decision you provide good reasons to support it.

> You must give evidence to justify your conclusions.

Kilo-

Kilo- is a prefix meaning 1000.

> A kilometre is 1000 metres.

▶ centi-, deca-, giga-, kilogram, kilometre, mega-, milli-

Kilogram (kg)

A kilogram is a measurement of weight or mass in the metric system, equal to 1000 grams.

> A bag of sugar weighs about 1 kilogram.

▶ gram, metric system

Kilometre (km)

A kilometre is a measurement of length in the metric system, equal to 1000 metres.

> It takes about 10 minutes to walk 1 kilometre.

▶ centimetre, metre, metric system, millimetre

Kite

A kite is a 4-sided polygon with two pairs of equal adjacent sides. One pair of opposite angles are equal and the diagonals of a kite intersect at right angles.

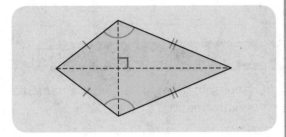

▶ adjacent, diagonal, opposite, polygon

A B C D E F G H I J K **L** M N O P Q R S T U V W X Y Z

L

KS2 1234

L is the symbol which stands for 50 in the Roman number system.

> LV is 55.

▶ C, D, I, M, Roman numerals, V, X

Label

KS1 📊

To label something is to give it a name to show information.

Each axis on a graph needs a label.

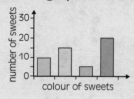

Latitude

KS2 🔲

Lines of latitude are imaginary circles drawn around the Earth, parallel to the equator. Together with lines of longitude they make a grid on the Earth's surface to help find exact positions.

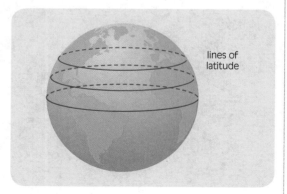

lines of latitude

▶ longitude

LCD

▶ lowest common denominator

LCM

▶ lowest common multiple

Leap year

KS2

A leap year is a calendar year of 366 days, with February having 29 days instead of 28. A leap year occurs every fourth year.

> 2016 and 2020 are leap years but 2018 is not as it is not divisible by 4.

▶ time, year

Least

KS1 ????

The least amount is the smallest quantity.

> A graph of favourite colours of a group of children will show the least popular colour.

Length

KS1

Length is the distance between two points or the two ends of a line. A length of time is the amount of time from the start of an event to its finish.

> ―――――――――
> The length of this line is 3 cm.

▶ breadth, width

Less than (<)

If one quantity is smaller than a second quantity then it is less than that second quantity.

> 0.35 < 0.5
>
> This shows that 0.35 is less than 0.5.

▶ greater than, more than

Line

A line is a straight or curved length with no width.

This is a curved line.

Line graph

A line graph is a graph where all the points are joined by straight lines.

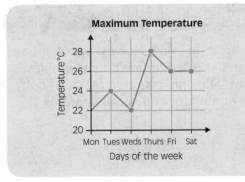

Maximum Temperature

▶ continuous data

Line of symmetry

A line of symmetry is a line about which a shape is symmetrical. If the shape is folded along the line, one half fits exactly over the other half.

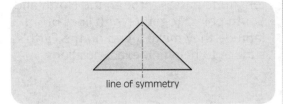

line of symmetry

▶ line symmetry, mirror line, reflection, symmetry

Line symmetry

A shape has line symmetry or reflection symmetry when two or more of its parts are matching shapes. If a mirror is placed along the line separating the two matching shapes, the shape looks unchanged.

▶ line of symmetry, mirror line, reflection, symmetry

Litre (l)

A litre (l) is a metric unit of capacity. There are 1000 millilitres in 1 litre.

A normal glass holds about one-third of a litre.

1 litre

▶ capacity, centilitre, millilitre

Longitude

Longitude is the distance in degrees east or west of the Greenwich Meridian at 0°. Lines of longitude are imaginary circles drawn around the Earth. Each line of longitude passes through the North and South poles. Together with lines of latitude they make a grid on the Earth's surface to help find exact positions.

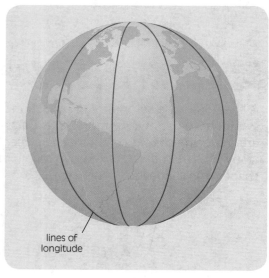

lines of longitude

▶ latitude

Loss

In business, to make a loss is to lose money on a deal and therefore not make a profit.

A garage made a loss last month because they bought some cars for more than they sold them.

▶ profit

Lowest common denominator (LCD)

The lowest common denominator (LCD) is the lowest common multiple of all the denominators in a set of fractions.

To put these in order of size, work out the LCD. $\frac{2}{3}$, $\frac{3}{4}$, $\frac{1}{6}$.

12 is the LCD of 3, 4 and 6:

$\frac{2}{3} = \frac{8}{12}$, $\frac{3}{4} = \frac{9}{12}$, $\frac{1}{6} = \frac{2}{12}$

so the order is $\frac{1}{6}$, $\frac{2}{3}$, $\frac{3}{4}$.

▶ denominator, fraction, lowest common multiple

Lowest common multiple (LCM)

The lowest common multiple (LCM) is the lowest number which is a multiple of two or more numbers.

The lowest common multiple of 3, 6 and 8 is 24.

▶ common multiple, multiple

Lowest terms

If a fraction is in its lowest terms, it has been cancelled until it is in its simplest form. The only common factor of both the numerator and denominator is 1.

$\frac{15}{20}$ in its lowest terms is $\frac{3}{4}$.

▶ cancel, denominator, numerator, reduce, simplify

M

KS2 1234

M is the symbol which stands for 1000 in the Roman number system.

MCM stands for 1900. This means 1000 plus 100 less than 1000, which is 1900.

▶ C, D, I, L, Roman numerals, V, X

Magic square

KS2 1234

A magic square is an arrangement of numbers in a square. If you add together all the numbers in any row, column or diagonal, the answer is the same.

6	1	8
7	5	3
2	9	4

Majority

KS2 1234

A majority of a group is more than half the items or people in that group.

In a survey about vegetables, the majority of the people preferred carrots to cabbage.

▶ minority

Mapping

KS2 xyz

A mapping changes something by following a given rule. Arrows are usually used to show a mapping.

The mappings 2 → 6, 5 → 15 and 8 → 24 have the rule 'multiply by 3'.

Mass

KS1

The mass of an object is the amount of material contained in it. The more massive an object is, the harder it is to make it move. In the metric system, mass is measured in grams and kilograms.

On Earth your mass and weight are the same, but your weight is affected by the pull of gravity. Your mass on the moon would be the same as on Earth but your weight would be different.

This pumpkin has a mass of 2 kg.

▶ weight

Maximum

KS1 1234

The maximum is the largest or greatest value or number in a set of numbers.

The maximum total with three 1–6 dice is 18.

▶ minimum

A
B
C
D
E
F
G
H
I
J
K
L
M
N
O
P
Q
R
S
T
U
V
W
X
Y
Z

Mean

The mean, or arithmetic mean, of a set of numbers is one way of working out an average. The mean is found by totalling all the numbers and dividing by how many numbers there are altogether.

> The mean of 3, 6, 8 and 7 is 6.
> $(3 + 6 + 8 + 7) \div 4 = 6$

▶ average, median, mode

Measure
KS1

To measure something is to find the size, quantity or degree of it.

> Tom measured the height of the gate.

▶ angle, area, capacity, length, mass, time

Measurement
KS1

A measurement is an amount or size discovered by measuring.

> The exact measurement of the mass of the parcel was 2.7 kg.

▶ angle, area, capacity, length, mass, time

Median
KS2

The median is the middle number in a set of numbers. It is one way of working out an average. The median is found by arranging all the numbers in order and finding the middle number.

> To find the median of 41 cm, 28 cm, 52 cm, 31 cm and 29 cm, write them in order:
>
> 28 cm, 29 cm, 31 cm, 41 cm, 52 cm
>
> The middle number, 31 cm, is the median.

▶ average, mean, mode

Mega-
KS2 1234

Mega- is a prefix meaning 1 000 000.

> Computer memory size can be measured in megabytes. A megabyte is one million bytes.

▶ centi-, deca-, giga-, kilo-, milli-

Method
KS1 ????

A method is a description of the way of doing a calculation or solving a problem.

> There are several mental methods for working out 39 + 84.

▶ calculation

Metre (m)

KS1

A metre is a measurement of length in the metric system.

There are 100 centimetres in 1 metre.

> A long stride is about one metre long.

▶ centimetre, kilometre, length, metric system

Metric system

KS1

The metric system is a system of weights and measures. All the units in the metric system are in tens, hundreds and thousands.

The metric system was developed in France in the 18th century. In 1897 a law was passed in the UK giving permission to use metric weights and measures.

> Millimetres, metres, litres, grams and kilograms are all examples of units in the metric system.

▶ imperial system

Midday

KS1

Midday is 12 o'clock in the middle of the day. Another word for midday is noon.

> Between midnight and midday, the time using the 12-hour clock is a.m. After midday up to midnight the time is p.m.

▶ a.m., o'clock, p.m., time

Midnight

KS1

Midnight is 12 o'clock in the middle of the night.

> The TV was set to record a film starting at midnight and finishing at 2.10 a.m.

Mile

KS2

A mile is an imperial measurement of length. There are 1760 yards in one mile.

The word mile comes from the Latin word *mille*, meaning one thousand. A mile was said to be the distance of 1000 paces.

> The one mile race is four laps of a 400 metre track.

▶ foot, imperial system, inch, yard

Millennium

KS2

A millennium is a period of 1000 years.

> We are now in the third millennium, which started on 1st January 2001.

Milli-

KS2

Milli- is a prefix meaning $\frac{1}{1000}$.

> A millilitre is one-thousandth of a litre.

▶ centi-, deca-, giga-, kilo-, mega-, metric system

Millilitre (ml)

KS2

A millilitre is a measurement of capacity equal to $\frac{1}{1000}$ litre. There are 1000 ml in 1 litre.

> 1 millilitre is a tiny amount. A teaspoon holds about 5 ml of liquid.

► capacity, centilitre, litre, metric system

Millimetre (mm)

KS2

A millimetre is a measurement of length equal to $\frac{1}{1000}$ of a metre. There are 10 mm in 1 cm.

> This line is 24 mm long

► centimetre, kilometre, metre, metric system

Million

KS2 1234

A million is the number 1 000 000. It is a very large number. If you counted to 1 million with a number every second, it would take you over 11 days.

> A million is one thousand thousand.

Minimum

KS1 1234

The minimum is the smallest or lowest value or number in a set of numbers.

> The minimum temperature reached last night was 2 °C.

► maximum

Minority

KS2 1234

A minority of a group is fewer than half the items or people in that group.

> Only a minority of players voted to change the colour of the football kit, so it remained blue.

► majority

Minuend

KS1

The first number in a subtraction, which then has an amount subtracted.

> $15 - 8 = 7$
>
> 15 is the minuend, 8 is the subtrahend, 7 is the difference.

► difference, subtraction, subtrahend

Minus (−)

KS1

You use minus to show that one number is being subtracted from another.

Minus is also sometimes used to say negative numbers, such as minus 5 for −5. It is actually better to say negative 5 so that it is not confused with the operation of subtraction. But we do use minus for temperatures. If the temperature is five degrees below zero we say that it is minus five degrees.

> 13 minus 7 is 6.

► subtraction, take away

Minute
KS1

A minute is a length of time. There are 60 seconds in one minute and 60 minutes in one hour.

> The second hand takes one minute to go around the watch once.

Mirror line
KS1

A mirror line is another name for a line of symmetry and is a line about which a shape is symmetrical. If a mirror is placed on the line, the half shape and its reflection show the whole shape.

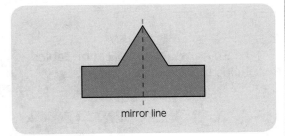

mirror line

▶ line of symmetry, reflection, symmetry

Mixed number
KS2 1234

A mixed number, or mixed fraction, is a whole number together with a proper fraction.

> $3\frac{2}{5}$ is a mixed number.

▶ improper fraction, proper fraction

Möbius strip
KS2

A Möbius strip is a flat strip of paper which is twisted halfway and the ends joined together. The shape is special as it has only one side and one edge.

The Möbius strip was invented in the 19th century by August Möbius, a German mathematician.

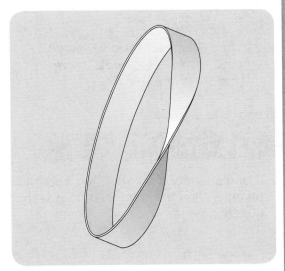

Mode
KS2

The mode is the most common number or item in a set of numbers or items. It is one way of finding an average.

> Shoe sizes for a group of children:
>
> 3, 4, 7, 5, 6, 3, 2, 6, 6, 4
>
> The mode for these shoe sizes is size 6.

▶ average, mean, median

Month KS1

A month has between 28 and 31 days and is approximately four weeks. It is the time it takes for the moon to go around the Earth once.

The length of a month is approximately equal to the time between one New Moon and the next New Moon, which is 29.5 days.

In the Gregorian calendar, used by most people in the world, there are 12 months in a year.

▶ day, leap year, year

More than (>) KS1

If one quantity is greater than a second quantity then it is more than that second quantity.

7 + 8 > 10

▶ greater than, less than

Multiple KS1

A multiple is a number made by multiplying together two other numbers. If one number divides exactly into another number, the second is a multiple of the first.

15 is a multiple of 5 because 3 × 5 is 15.

All multiples of 5 end in 0 or 5.

▶ common multiple, lowest common multiple

Multiplicand KS1

A number that is multiplied by another number. The multiplicand and multiplier are more commonly called factors.

6 × 4 = 24

6 is the multiplicand, 4 is the multiplier and 24 is the product.

▶ factor, multiple, multiplier, product

Multiplication (×) KS1

Multiplication is the operation of adding a number to itself a given number of times (repeated addition) or of scaling one number by another. With multiplication you multiply two numbers together. Multiplication is commutative, associative and distributive over addition or subtraction.

Learning your multiplication tables helps to speed up calculations.

Multiplicative reasoning KS2

Using the processes of multiplication and division to solve problems and think mathematically.

Multiplicative reasoning would be needed to solve this problem:

A coat costing £45 was reduced in a sale by 20%. What was the cost of the coat in the sale?

▶ division, multiplication

Multiplier

KS1

A number that multiplies another number. The multiplicand and multiplier are more commonly called factors.

> $12 \times 6 = 72$
>
> 12 is the multiplicand, 6 is the multiplier and 72 is the product.

▶ factor, multiple, multiplicand, product

Multiply

KS1

Multiply means to carry out the process of multiplication. To multiply is to increase a number in size by scaling it up, making it a number of times bigger. Multiplying is also the process of repeatedly adding a number to itself a given number of times.

> $5 \times 4 = 20$
>
> 5 multiplied by 4 or 5 times 4 can be calculated by adding 5 four times:
>
> $5 + 5 + 5 + 5 = 20$

▶ multiplication

A
B
C
D
E
F
G
H
I
J
K
L
M
N
O
P
Q
R
S
T
U
V
W
X
Y
Z

Narrow

Narrow means thin, or of small width.

> Sam cut a narrow strip from a piece of card, 1.5 cm wide.

► breadth, width

Natural number

Natural numbers are the set of positive numbers, as used in counting. Zero can be included or not – it is a matter of choice.

> 1, 2, 3, 4, 5, 6 … are all natural numbers.

► integer, whole number

Nautical mile

A nautical mile is a measurement of length used at sea. It is equal to 1852 metres.

> 1 knot is a unit of speed of one nautical mile per hour.

Nearest

The nearest is the closest whole number or multiple of ten, used when rounding.

> 38.7 is 39 rounded to the nearest whole number.

► round, whole number

Negative number

A number less than zero is a negative number. The minus sign (–) is used to show when a number is negative.

> –14, –8, and –25 are all negative numbers.

► minus, positive number, zero

Net

A net is a flat shape made from polygons that can be folded and joined to make into a polyhedron.

> This is a net of a cube.
>
>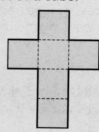

Nonagon

A nonagon is a polygon with nine straight sides.

This is a regular nonagon.

► polygon

North

KS1

North is one of the four main points of the compass, opposite to south.

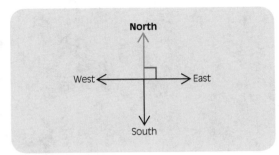

▶ compass, east, south, west

Nought

KS1 1234

Nought is an old word meaning nothing or zero. It is written as the digit 0. Nowadays we use the word zero more often in mathematics.

If you take seven away from seven you are left with nought.

▶ zero

Number

KS1 1234

A number is a symbol used for counting.

We use the digits 0, 1, 2, 3, 4, 5, 6, 7, 8 and 9 to make our numbers.

▶ digit

Number bond

KS1 +−×÷

Number bonds are pairs of numbers that make a particular total.

The number bonds for 8 are 0 + 8, 1 + 7, 2 + 6, 3 + 5 and 4 + 4.

Number line

KS1 1234

A number line is a line with a scale showing numbers in order.

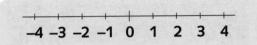

▶ number track

Number sentence

KS1 +−×÷

A number sentence is a statement used in mathematics which has numbers instead of words.

4 + 8 = 12 is a number sentence.

Number square

KS1 1234

A number track arranged into a square grid, keeping the numbers in order.

1	2	3	4
5	6	7	8
9	10	11	12
13	14	15	16

▶ number track

Number track

KS1
`1234`

A number track is a track with numbers in it, with each number in a region along the track representing the number of single moves from the start. Unlike a number line, there is no value between each number along the track.

1	2	3	4	5	6	7	8	9	10

▶ number line, number square

Numeral

KS1
`1234`

A numeral is a word or a figure written down to represent a number.

Five, 5 and V are all numerals for the same number.

Numerator

KS2
`½ 0.5 50%`

The numerator is the number above the line in a fraction. The number below the line, the denominator, shows you the number of equal parts. The numerator tells you how many of these equal parts you are using.

In the fraction $\frac{3}{4}$, the numerator is 3.
$\frac{3}{4}$ of 20 is 15.
$(20 \div 4) \times 3 = 15$

▶ denominator, fraction

Oblique
KS2

An oblique line is a line that is sloping or slanted.

> A diagonal is an oblique line across a shape from one corner to another.

Oblong
KS1

An oblong is a rectangle in which one pair of opposite sides is longer than the other pair.

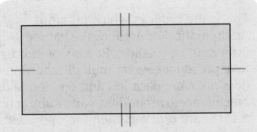

> Oblongs and squares are both types of rectangles.

▶ rectangle

Obtuse angle
KS2

An obtuse angle is an angle bigger than a right angle (90°) but smaller than a straight line (180°).

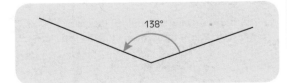

▶ acute angle, reflex angle, right angle

O'clock
KS1

Used after the numbers 1 to 12 to give the time on the hour.

> The clock shows 7 o'clock.

Octagon
KS1

An octagon is a polygon with eight straight sides.

> This is a regular octagon.

▶ polygon

Octahedron
KS2

An octahedron is a polyhedron with eight flat faces. A regular octahedron has eight faces that are equilateral triangles.

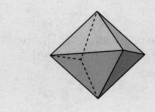

▶ equilateral triangle, face, polyhedron

Odd number • Order of operation

Odd number
KS1 1234

When a number is divided by 2 and gives a remainder of 1, it is an odd number.

> All odd numbers end with the digits 1, 3, 5, 7 or 9. So 4027 is an odd number.

▶ divide, even number, remainder

Operation
KS1 +−×÷

A rule or method for changing numbers in a calculation is an operation.

> The four basic number operations are addition, subtraction, multiplication and division.

▶ addition, calculation, division, multiplication, order of operation, subtraction

Opposite
KS1 ????

1. Something that is completely different is the opposite.

> Addition is the opposite of subtraction.

2. To be in a position opposite something is to be facing it.

> In an isosceles triangle, the two equal angles are opposite the two equal sides.

Order
KS1 1234

When you arrange items or numbers in a sequence so that each one is greater or smaller than the previous one, you are putting them in order.

> 17, 21, 28, 31, 42, 44
>
> These numbers are written in order of increasing size.

▶ ascending, decrease, descending, increase

Order of operation
KS2 +−×÷

This is the order in which different mathematical operations are carried out when calculating. Powers or indices take precedence over multiplication or division. Multiplication and division take precedence over addition and subtraction. If there are brackets then the operation inside the brackets takes precedence over the others.

> BIDMAS is a common mnemonic to remember the order of operations:
>
> Brackets
>
> Indices
>
> Division and Multiplication
>
> Addition and Subtraction

▶ addition, brackets, division, index, multiplication, operation, subtraction

Order of rotational symmetry

KS2

The order of rotational symmetry of a shape is the number of times that it can be turned to fit on to itself until it comes back to its original position.

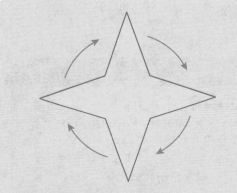

This star has an order of rotational symmetry of 4.

Ordinal number

KS1

Ordinal numbers are numbers used to describe the position of an object in a set, when they are put in order.

First (1st), second (2nd), third (3rd) and fourth (4th) are all ordinal numbers.

▶ first, second

Origin

KS2

The origin is the point on a graph where the two axes cross. The coordinates for the origin are (0, 0).

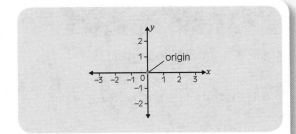

▶ axis, coordinate, *x*-axis, *y*-axis

Ounce (oz)

KS2

An ounce (oz) is an imperial unit of mass or weight. There are 16 ounces in a pound (lb). 1 ounce is approximately 28 g.

A slice of bread weighs about two ounces.

▶ imperial system, mass, pound, ton

Oval

KS2

An oval is a flat egg-shape or an ellipse.

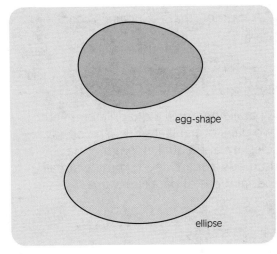

egg-shape

ellipse

▶ ellipse

Pair
KS1 1234

A pair is a set of two things.

> A trapezium has one pair of parallel sides.

Palindrome
KS2 1234

A palindrome is a number that is the same when it is read forwards as it is when it is read backwards. A word can also be palindromic, such as 'level'.

> 28182 and 34543 are both palindromes.

Parallel
KS2 ○△□

Lines that are parallel always stay the same distance apart and never meet.

> A rhombus has two pairs of parallel sides.

Parallelogram
KS2 ○△□

A parallelogram is a quadrilateral with two pairs of parallel sides. The opposite sides are also equal in length. The rhombus, square and rectangle are all special types of parallelograms.

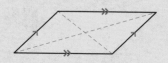

▶ polygon, quadrilateral, rectangle, rhombus, square

Partition
KS1 1234

Partitioning involves separating a set into subsets. When a number is partitioned it is split into separate parts.

> The number 65 can be partitioned in different ways, including 60 and 5, 50 and 15, or 30 and 35.

▶ complement, set

Pattern
KS1 ????

A pattern is a special arrangement of numbers or shapes. Patterns repeat or change in a regular way.

> 0, 5, 10, 15, 20, 25, 30 …
>
> The five times table has a special pattern.

▶ sequence

Penny (p) (plural: pence)
KS1 1234

A penny is a unit of money in the UK. There are 100 pence in one pound.

> This costs 34 pence.
>
>

▶ currency, pound

Pentagon

A pentagon is a polygon with five straight sides.

This is a regular pentagon.

▶ dodecahedron, polygon

Pentahedron

A pentahedron is a polyhedron with five flat faces. A square-based pyramid is called a pentahedron.

A square-based pyramid has 5 plane faces and is a pentahedron.

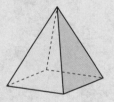

▶ base, face, polyhedron, pyramid, square

Per cent (%)

Per cent is another way of writing a fraction out of 100.
One hundred per cent (100%) is the whole, 50% is the same as $\frac{50}{100}$ or $\frac{1}{2}$.

In a sale, the trainers were reduced by 50% from £42 to £21.

▶ fraction, percentage

Percentage

A percentage is a fraction out of 100. You divide something into 100 parts to make a percentage.

The percentage of diamonds in a pack of cards is one quarter or 25%.

▶ fraction, per cent

Perfect number

A number that is the sum of its factors (apart from itself) is a perfect number.

6 is a perfect number:
$1 + 2 + 3 = 6$

28 is a perfect number:
$1 + 2 + 4 + 7 + 14 = 28$

Perimeter

The perimeter is the edge or boundary of an area. It is also the length of that edge.

The perimeter of a rectangle is found by adding the lengths of all the sides.

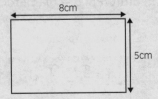

The perimeter is:
8 cm + 8 cm + 5 cm + 5 cm = 26 cm

▶ area, circumference, edge

Perpendicular

KS2

A perpendicular line is one at right angles to another line.

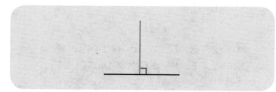

▶ parallel, right angle

Pi (π)

KS2

Pi is the ratio of the circumference of a circle to the length of its diameter. If the circumference of a circle is divided by its diameter, the answer is always equal to pi. Pi is just over 3, but can never be worked out exactly. It is approximately 3.1415926 but the digits after the decimal point go on for ever.

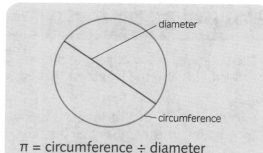

$$\pi = \text{circumference} \div \text{diameter}$$

▶ circle, circumference, diameter

Pictogram

KS1

A chart using pictures or symbols to represent numbers of items is a pictogram or pictograph. Each symbol stands for a certain number of items. The meaning of the symbols is shown by a key.

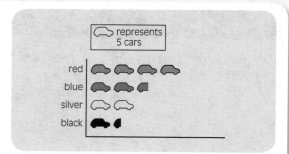

| represents 5 cars |
| red |
| blue |
| silver |
| black |

Pie chart

KS2

A pie chart is a circular chart that shows how something is shared out or divided up. The sectors within the circle represent the quantities, which are proportional to the angle at the centre of the circle.

This pie chart shows that more red cars than blue cars passed a school one morning.

Colours of cars

Pint (pt)

KS2

A pint is an imperial unit of capacity. There are eight pints in 1 gallon. 1 pint is just over 0.5 litres.

Milk bottles hold 1 pint of milk.

▶ capacity, gallon, imperial system

Place holder

KS2 `1234`

The numeral zero (0) is used as a place holder to show that there is no value for a particular place in a decimal number.

37.05 has a zero in the $\frac{1}{10}$ position to show that the number is:

$30 + 7 + \frac{0}{10} + \frac{5}{100}$

Place value

KS1 `1234`

The place value is the position or place of a digit in a number. The same digit has a different value at different places in the number.

In the number 384, the place value of 3 is 300, 8 is 80 and 4 is 4.

$300 + 80 + 4 = 384$

► digit, position

Plan

KS2

A plan is a scale drawing or design for an object or building.

This is the plan for a new office.

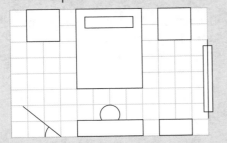

Plane

KS2

A plane is a flat surface. Plane shapes are flat shapes with length and width but no thickness. They are two-dimensional shapes.

This polygon is a plane shape.

► polygon, two-dimensional

Plot

KS2

When you plot points on a graph you mark the position of given coordinates.

Position (3, 4) has been plotted.

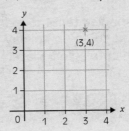

Plus (+)

KS1 `+−×÷`

Plus means add or in addition to.

7 plus 12 equals 19.

$7 + 12 = 19$

► addition

p.m. **KS2**

The short way of writing 'post meridiem' is p.m., which means after midday or noon.

> Sam went to bed at 8.35 p.m.

▶ a.m., midday

Point **KS2** ????

A point is a dot or mark showing a position on a graph or where lines cross.

> The line was drawn through each point.

▶ graph, position

Poll **KS2**

A poll is a survey of people's opinions or intentions.

> A poll showed that more people preferred going on holiday to a hot place than to a cold place.

Polygon **KS1** ○△□

A polygon is a flat or plane shape with many straight sides. If a polygon has sides of equal length and angles that are equal it is said to be a regular polygon.

> A square and an equilateral triangle are examples of regular polygons.

▶ hexagon, pentagon, quadrilateral, regular, triangle

Polyhedron (plural: polyhedra) **KS2** ○△□

A polyhedron is a many-sided solid shape with faces made from polygons. The faces of polyhedra meet at their edges and the edges meet at points called vertices.

▶ edge, face, polygon, vertex

Population **KS2**

The number of people that live in a certain place is its population.

> The population of the UK is approximately 60 million.

Portion **KS1** 1234

A portion is a piece or part of a whole.

> If a cake is divided into five equal portions, each portion is $\frac{1}{5}$ of the whole.

▶ division

Position • Prime number

Position

KS1

1. The position of an object is its place or location. Position can also mean the order in which things are placed.

   The top three positions in a race are 1st, 2nd and 3rd.

▶ ordinal number

2. When you put something in a certain place you position it.

   Emma positioned the pieces on the board to begin the game of chess.

Positive number

KS2 1234

A number greater than zero is a positive number. The plus sign (+) is sometimes used to show when a number is positive.

   3, 18 and 40 are all positive numbers.

▶ negative number, zero

Pound

KS2

1. A pound (lb) is an imperial unit of weight or mass. There are 16 ounces in a pound and 14 pounds in a stone. 1 kilogram is approximately 2.2 lb.

   Four apples weigh about a pound.

▶ imperial system, kilogram, mass, ounce, stone

2. A pound (£) is a unit of money in the UK. 100 pence is equal to £1.

   Three packets of crisps cost about £1.

▶ currency, penny

Power

▶ index

Price

KS1 1234

The price of something is how much it costs or its expense.

   In a sale, the price of a tennis racket was reduced to £15.

Prime factor

KS2 1234

A prime factor is a factor that is a prime number.

   The factors of 12 are 1, 2, 3, 4, 6 and 12. The prime factors are 2 and 3.

▶ factor, prime number

Prime number

KS2 1234

A prime number is any whole number, apart from 1, that can only be divided by itself and by 1 without leaving a remainder. Another way of saying this is that a prime number only has two factors, 1 and itself.

   The first four prime numbers are 2, 3, 5 and 7.

▶ factor, remainder

A B C D E F G H I J K L M N O P Q R S T U V W X Y Z

Prism

KS1

A prism is a polyhedron with matching ends. The ends are polygons, such as triangles, squares or hexagons. A prism has the same cross-section all the way along its length.

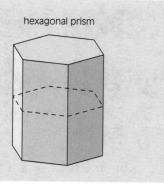

hexagonal prism

► cross-section, polygon, polyhedron

Product

KS1

When two or more numbers are multiplied together, the answer is the product of those numbers.

The product of 3 and 5 is 15.

$3 \times 5 = 15$

► multiply

Profit

KS2
1234

In business, to make a profit is to make money on a deal.

A profit was made when they sold the house because they sold it for more money than they bought it.

► loss

Proper fraction

KS2

A proper fraction has a value less than 1. The numerator is smaller than the denominator.

$\frac{7}{8}$ is a proper fraction.

► denominator, fraction, numerator, unit fraction

Property

KS1
????

A property of a shape or number is a particular fact or feature of it that makes it part of a group with the same properties.

It is a property of square numbers that they have an odd number of factors.

Proportion

KS2

Finding the proportion of an amount is the same as finding the fraction of the whole amount. A proportion can be written as a fraction.

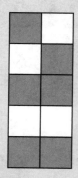

The proportion of squares that are red is $\frac{6}{10}$ or $\frac{3}{5}$.

► fraction, ratio

A B C D E F G H I J K L M N O P Q R S T U V W X Y Z

Protractor

A protractor is an instrument used for measuring angles. It has a scale that is marked in degrees.

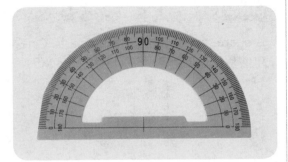

▶ angle, degree

Pyramid

A pyramid is a polyhedron with a polygon base and triangular faces that meet at one of the vertices called an apex. The base of a pyramid can be any polygon, such as a triangle, a square or a hexagon, and these are used to name the pyramid.

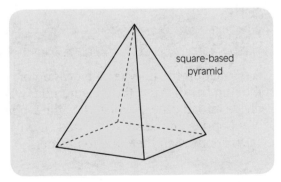

square-based pyramid

▶ base, face, polygon, polyhedron, vertex

Quadrant
KS2

1. A quadrant is one-quarter of a circle.

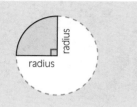

2. A quadrant is the name given to each of the four areas on a graph or coordinates grid. The graph is divided into four quadrants by its axes.

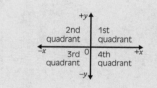

Quadrilateral
KS1

A quadrilateral is a polygon with four sides.

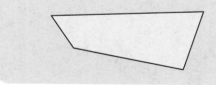

▶ arrowhead, kite, parallelogram, polygon, rectangle, rhombus, square, trapezium

Quadruple
KS2 1234

1. When you quadruple something you multiply it by four.

If you have £6 and it is quadrupled, you will have £24.

2. Four times a number is its quadruple.

24 is quadruple 6.

▶ double, triple

Quarter
KS1

A quarter is one of four equal parts. One-quarter ($\frac{1}{4}$) is one-fourth part of a whole.

$\frac{1}{4}$	$\frac{1}{4}$
$\frac{1}{4}$	$\frac{1}{4}$

▶ fraction, half, quadrant

Questionnaire
KS2

A questionnaire is a sheet of questions used to collect data.

The class made up a questionnaire about the leisure activities of the pupils in their school.

▶ data

Quotient
KS2

A quotient is the answer to a division or the number of times that one number will divide into another number. It is the whole number part of the answer to a division calculation when there are remainders.

$25 \div 2 = 12.5$

The quotient is 12.5.

$25 \div 2 = 12$ remainder 1

The quotient is 12.

▶ division, remainder

Radius (plural radii)

KS2

The radius is the length of a straight line from the centre of a circle to its circumference.

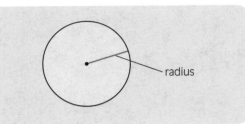

radius

▶ centre, circle, circumference, diameter

Range

KS2

The range is the spread of data; it is the difference between the greatest and least values.

The heights of a group of children ranged from 132 cm to 154 cm. The range was 22 cm.

▶ average, mean, median, mode

Rate

KS2

Rate is a measure of how quickly one amount changes in comparison to another amount.

Speed is a rate that measures how distance travelled changes over time.

Ratio

KS2

Ratio compares one part or amount with another.

The ratio of white to red squares is 4 to 6 or 2 to 3. For every 2 white squares there are 3 red squares. This is written as 2:3.

▶ proportion

Rational number

KS2
1234

A rational number is a number that can be written as $\frac{a}{b}$ where a and b are both integers and the denominator is not zero.

$3, \frac{2}{3}, \frac{9}{10}, 6.5, 245$ are all rational numbers.

▶ irrational number

Rectangle

KS1

A rectangle is a four-sided polygon. It has two pairs of opposite, equal parallel sides and each angle is a right angle (90°). A rectangle is a parallelogram with 90° angles. A square is a rectangle with equal length sides. A rectangle that is not square is also known as an oblong.

▶ oblong, polygon, quadrilateral, square

A B C D E F G H I J K L M N O P Q R S T U V W X Y Z

Rectilinear
KS2

A rectilinear shape is a polygon that can be divided into rectangles, squares and triangles so that the area of the shape can be calculated.

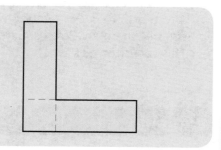

Recurring decimal
KS2 1234

Recurring means repeating. A recurring decimal has digits that are in a repeated pattern, like 0.33333 … or 0.252525 ….

On your calculator, the calculation 2 ÷ 3 gives the answer 0.6666666. This is 'zero point six recurring' which is sometimes written as 0.6̇.

▶ decimal

Reduce
KS2 ½ 0.5 50%

To reduce is to make smaller in size. A fraction is reduced by cancelling or simplifying it to its lowest terms. This is carried out by dividing the numerator and denominator by a common factor.

$\frac{12}{18}$ is reduced to $\frac{2}{3}$ in its lowest terms.

▶ cancel, lowest terms, simplify

Reflection
KS1

A reflection is an image seen in a mirror. A shape with two sides that are mirror images has reflection or line symmetry.

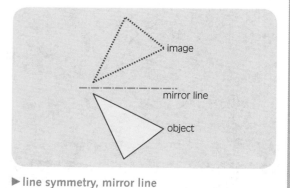

▶ line symmetry, mirror line

Reflective symmetry
KS1

A shape has reflective symmetry or line symmetry when two or more of its parts are matching shapes. If a mirror is placed along the line separating the two matching shapes, the shape looks unchanged.

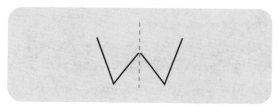

▶ line symmetry, symmetry

Reflex angle
KS2

A reflex angle is an angle greater than 180°.

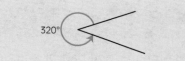

▶ acute angle, obtuse angle, right angle

Regular

KS2

A regular polygon has sides of equal length and angles of equal size.

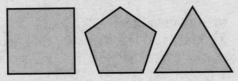

These are all regular polygons.

▶ irregular, polygon

Relationship

KS1
$x\ y\ z$

When you look for a relationship between sets of numbers, you look for the way they are connected, often with a rule.

$3 \rightarrow 6$, $8 \rightarrow 16$, $5 \rightarrow 10$

The relationship arrows all show 'is half of'.

▶ function

Remainder

KS2
$+-\times\div$

If a number cannot be divided exactly by another number, then there is a whole number answer with a remainder or an amount left over.

When you divide 23 by 4, the quotient is 5 with a remainder of 3.

$23 \div 4 = 5$ remainder 3

▶ division, quotient

Repeated addition

KS1
$+-\times\div$

Repeated addition is a model for multiplication by repeatedly adding the same amount.

$4 + 4 + 4 + 4 + 4 = 4 \times 5$

Repeated subtraction

KS1
$+-\times\div$

Repeated subtraction is a model for division by repeatedly subtracting the same amount.

$15 - 5 - 5 - 5 = 0$

So $15 \div 5 = 3$

Represent

KS2
$x\ y\ z$

A symbol or letter can be used to represent numbers.

In the formula $A = l \times b$, A represents area, l represents length and b represents breadth.

▶ area, breadth, formula, length

Revolution

KS2

A revolution is a complete turn through 360°.

Four right angles make one complete revolution.

▶ circle, right angle

A B C D E F G H I J K L M N O P Q R S T U V W X Y Z

A B C D E F G H I J K L M N O P Q R S T U V W X Y Z

Rhombus

KS2

A rhombus is a special parallelogram. It is a polygon with four equal sides but no right angles. It is sometimes called a diamond.

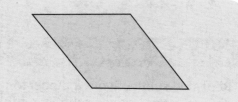

▶ parallelogram, polygon, quadrilateral

Right angle

KS2

An angle of 90 degrees (90°) is called a right angle. It is a quarter of a revolution.

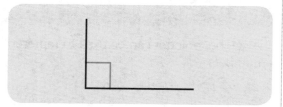

▶ acute angle, obtuse angle, perpendicular, reflex angle, revolution

Right-angled triangle

KS2

A right-angled triangle has one angle of 90 degrees (90°).

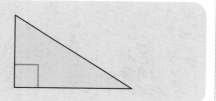

▶ equilateral triangle, isosceles triangle, right angle, scalene triangle

Roman numerals

KS2 1234

Roman numerals are a number system used by the ancient Romans. They used different capital letters for ones, tens, hundreds and thousands and had no symbol for zero.

In Roman numerals 99 is XCIX. XC means 10 less than 100 (90) and IX is one less than ten (9). This is put together to make 99.

▶ C, D, I, L, M, V, X

Rotate

KS1

To rotate is to turn around. When a shape is rotated it is turned around a centre of rotation either clockwise or anticlockwise.

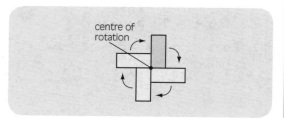

centre of rotation

▶ centre of rotation, rotational symmetry

Rotational symmetry

KS2

A shape has rotational symmetry if there are a number of positions the shape can take when rotated, and still look the same.

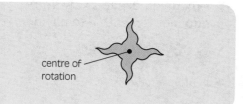

centre of rotation

▶ centre of rotation, rotate, symmetry

Round

KS1

1. Round means shaped like a circle.

CDs are round.

► circle

KS2
1234

2. To round a whole number means to change it to the nearest ten, hundred or thousand to give an approximate number and to make it easier to work with. Decimal numbers can be rounded to the nearest whole number, tenth or hundredth.

74 684 is 75 000 rounded to the nearest 1000.

8.2791 is 8.3 rounded to the nearest tenth.

► decimal, hundredth, tenth, whole number

Row

KS1
1234

A row is a horizontal arrangement of objects or numbers going across.

1	2	3	4
5	6	7	8
9	10	11	12

The numbers in the middle row are 5, 6, 7 and 8.

► column

Ruler

KS1

A ruler is a straight-edged instrument with a scale marked along it. It is used to draw and measure straight lines.

► measure, scale

A
B
C
D
E
F
G
H
I
J
K
L
M
N
O
P
Q
R
S
T
U
V
W
X
Y
Z

Scale

1. A scale is a marked measuring line.

If you read the scale you will see that this jug has 600 ml of liquid in it.

▶ measure

2. A scale for a drawing or map gives its size compared to the real thing. It is the ratio of the drawn distance to its actual value.

Some road maps have a scale of 1 cm representing 2 km.

▶ mapping, ratio

Scalene triangle

A scalene triangle has no equal sides or angles.

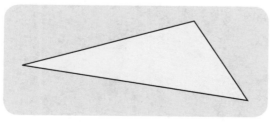

▶ equilateral triangle, isosceles triangle, right-angled triangle

Schedule

A schedule is a timetable or a timed plan for a project.

According to the schedule for our school trips, our next visit is to the museum.

Score

A score is a word for the number 20.

The word score comes from an old Saxon word *Sceran* meaning to cut. It is thought that a notch was cut into a tally stick each time a group of twenty was recorded.

He lived for 3 score years and 10. (He lived for 70 years.)

Second

1. An ordinal number, the second (2nd) position is the one following the first (1st).

February is the second month in the year.

▶ first

2. A second is an amount of time (sec). There are 60 seconds in 1 minute.

It takes about 1 second to say the word 'second'.

▶ hour, minute, time

Sector
KS2

A sector is a section of a circle. It is like taking a slice from a circle by making two cuts from the centre.

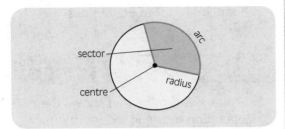

▶ arc, centre, chord, circle, radius

Segment
KS2

A segment of a circle is like a piece taken off the circle with a single cut.

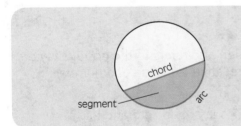

▶ circle

Semicircle
KS1

A semicircle is half a circle.

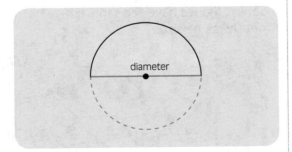

▶ circle, diameter

Sequence
KS1 1234

A sequence is a row of numbers. The next number in a sequence is found by applying a rule to the previous number.

In the sequence 1, 5, 9, 13, 17, 21 … the rule is +4. The next two numbers will be 25 and 29.

▶ Fibonacci sequence, pattern

Set
KS1 1234

A set is a group of numbers, shapes or objects with a particular thing in common.

The set of odd numbers between 0 and 10 is 1, 3, 5, 7 and 9.

▶ Carroll diagram, sort, Venn diagram

Set square
KS2

A set square is an instrument shaped like a right-angled triangle. It is used for drawing parallel and perpendicular lines.

▶ parallel, perpendicular, right-angled triangle

Shape
KS1

A shape is a figure made up of drawn lines. In mathematics, shapes are drawn with lines to show their edges or sides. Plane shapes are flat, two-dimensional shapes and solid shapes are three-dimensional.

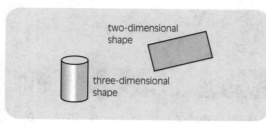

two-dimensional shape

three-dimensional shape

▶ polygon, polyhedron, three-dimensional, two-dimensional

Share
KS1

1. A share of something is a portion or part of a whole amount.

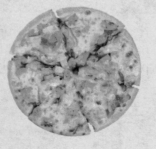

This pizza has been cut up into 6 shares.

2. To share is to divide equally between two or more people.

If 24 sweets are shared equally between three people, each person will get eight sweets.

▶ divide

Side
KS1

A side of a shape is the line that forms part of the edge or perimeter.

A square has four equal sides.

Sign
KS1

1. A sign is a symbol that shows the operation to use in a calculation.

+, −, × and ÷ are the signs for addition, subtraction, multiplication and division.

▶ calculate, symbol

KS1

2. Sign also refers to the positive (+) or negative (−) value of a number.

−4 is less than zero and has a negative sign.

▶ negative number, positive number

Similar figure
KS2

Similar figures have the same shape but not the same size.

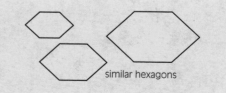

similar hexagons

▶ congruent

Simplify

KS1 ½ 0.5 50%

A fraction is simplified by reducing it to its lowest terms. Dividing the numerator and denominator by the same number will simplify a fraction.

$\frac{15}{21}$ can be simplified by dividing numerator and denominator by 3.

$\frac{15}{21} = \frac{5}{7}$

▶ cancel, denominator, lowest terms, numerator, reduce

Single

KS1 1234

A single item is one that is on its own, separate from all the others.

There was a single apple left in the bowl.

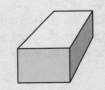

Solid figure

KS1 ○△□

If an object has three dimensions it is known as a solid figure or polyhedron. It has length, breadth and height.

This cuboid is a solid figure.

▶ polyhedron, three-dimensional

Solution

KS1 +−×÷

The solution to a problem is the answer or result.

I'm thinking of a number. If I halve it and add 3, I make 9. What is my number? The solution to this problem is 12.

Sort

KS1

To sort is to collect objects and numbers into different groups depending on chosen rules. The groups are known as sets.

Shapes can be sorted into sets of shapes with curved edges and straight edges.

▶ Carroll diagram, set, Venn diagram

South

KS1

South is one of the four main points of the compass, opposite to north.

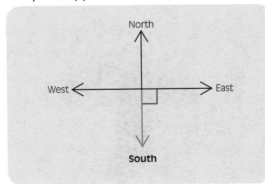

▶ compass, east, north, west

A B C D E F G H I J K L M N O P Q R S T U V W X Y Z

Space

All objects take up space. The amount of space objects fill depends on their size or volume.

> Capacity is the amount of space in a container.

▶ capacity, volume

Speed

Speed tells you how fast something is moving. It is how far something moves in a certain amount of time.

> The car travelled at a speed of 70 kilometres per hour (kph). In three hours it travelled 210 kilometres.

Sphere

A sphere is a solid shape with a curved surface. All the points on the surface of a sphere are exactly the same distance from its centre.

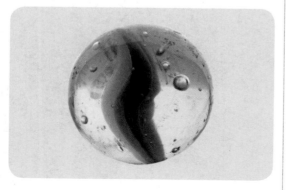

▶ centre, curve, polyhedron

Spherical

A spherical object is an object shaped like a sphere such as a ball.

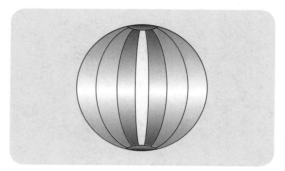

▶ sphere

Square

1. A square is a quadrilateral with four straight and equal sides. The angles in its corners are all right angles.

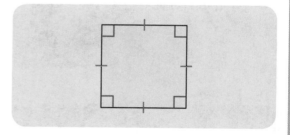

▶ quadrilateral

2. To square a number is to multiply it by itself. You can show that a number is squared by writing a small number 2 just after and above the number, e.g. 5^2.

> 5 squared is $5^2 = 5 \times 5 = 25$.

▶ index, multiply, square number

Square-based pyramid

▶ pyramid

Square centimetre (cm²) `KS2`

A square centimetre is a unit of area – a square measuring 1 cm × 1 cm.

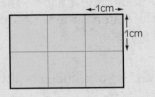

This shape has an area of 6 cm².

▶ area, centimetre, metric system

Square metre (m²) `KS2`

A square metre is a unit of area – a square measuring 1 m × 1 m.

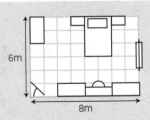

This room has an area of 48 m².

▶ area, hectare, metre, metric system

Square number `KS2` `1234`

A square number is formed when a number is multiplied by itself. A square number can be arranged as a group of dots in the shape of a square. The number of dots is the same as the number itself. The first four square numbers are 1, 4, 9 and 16.

$1^2 = 1$, $2^2 = 4$, $3^2 = 9$, $4^2 = 16$

▶ index, square

Square root (√) `KS2` `1234`

The square root of a number is the number that, when multiplied by itself, gives you the first number. 3 is the square root of 9. When 3 is squared (3 × 3) the answer is 9.

The square root of 49 is 7.

$\sqrt{49} = 7$

▶ square

Statistics `KS2`

Statistics are a collection of data or information which are displayed and analysed.

The statistics showed that the taller the person, the longer their arms.

Stone `KS2`

A stone is an imperial unit of weight. There are 14 pounds in a stone. 1 stone weighs just over 6 kilograms.

An average man weighs about 13 stone.

▶ imperial system, ounce, pound

A B C D E F G H I J K L M N O P Q R S T U V W X Y Z

Straight line

KS1

A straight line is the shortest distance between two points. It is a line that joins two points without bending.

A •————————• B

This is a straight line between A and B.

Subtraction (−)

KS1
+−×÷

Subtraction means taking one number away from another. The − sign shows that one number is being subtracted from another.

Subtract 15 from 20.

20 − 15 = 5

► difference, take away

Subtrahend

KS1
+−×÷

The quantity subtracted from another quantity is the subtrahend.

70 − 30 = 40

70 is the minuend, 30 is the subtrahend, 40 is the difference.

► minuend, subtraction

Sum

KS1
+−×÷

The sum of two or more numbers is the answer you get when you add them together.

The sum of the first three even numbers is 12.

2 + 4 + 6 = 12

► addition, total

Surface

KS1

The surface of an object is its outside layer or boundary. It has no thickness. The surface area is the total area of the outside surface.

The surface of a cube consists of six square faces.

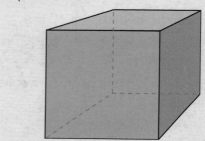

Survey

KS2

Carrying out a survey involves collecting data so that it can be displayed and analysed.

The class carried out a traffic survey to analyse the road use outside their school.

► data

Symbol

KS1 1234

A mark or sign standing for something is known as a symbol. There are many mathematical symbols, including numbers (1, 2, 3, 4 …), signs (+, −, ×, ÷) and notation (<, >, =, %).

> The symbols for greater than and less than are > and <.

Symmetrical

KS1 ○△□

A symmetrical shape is one that is balanced about a point, line or plane.

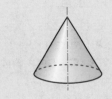

Symmetry

KS1 ○△□

A shape has symmetry when two or more of its parts are matching shapes. If a figure keeps its shape when reflected or rotated it is said to have symmetry.

> The letter A has line symmetry and the letter Z has rotational symmetry.

▶ line symmetry, rotational symmetry

A
B
C
D
E
F
G
H
I
J
K
L
M
N
O
P
Q
R
S
T
U
V
W
X
Y
Z

A
B
C
D
E
F
G
H
I
J
K
L
M
N
O
P
Q
R
S
T
U
V
W
X
Y
Z

Table **KS1**

A table is a list of numbers or information in rows and columns.

×	1	2	3
1	1	2	3
2	2	4	6
3	3	6	9

▶ column, row

Take away (–) **KS1** $+ - × ÷$

To take away is to remove items or numbers from an amount. The – sign shows that one number is being taken away from another.

16 take away 7 equals 9.

$16 - 7 = 9$

▶ difference, subtraction

Tally **KS1**

To tally is to count by making marks. The most common method is to mark off sets of 5.

Car colour	Tally	Frequency
red	⌷⌷⌷⌷ ⌷⌷⌷⌷ II	12
blue	⌷⌷⌷⌷ II	7
white	III	3
total		22

Tangram **KS2**

A tangram is a Chinese puzzle in which a square is cut into five triangles, one square and one parallelogram. The shapes are then used to make different figures.

Temperature **KS1**

Temperature is a measure of how hot or how cold something is. Temperature is measured in degrees (°) as a number on a scale. The most common temperature scales are the Celsius (°C) scale and the Fahrenheit (°F) scale.

The temperature rose by 8 °C today, reaching a maximum of 24 °C.

▶ Celsius, climate, Fahrenheit

Tenth (10th) **KS1** 1234

1. The tenth thing is the one after the ninth if they are put in order.

October is the tenth month in the year.

▶ hundredth, ordinal number

KS2

2. A tenth ($\frac{1}{10}$) is a fraction. One-tenth is one out of ten parts.

A millimetre is a tenth of a centimetre.

▶ decimal, fraction, half, quarter

Tessellation

A tessellation is a pattern made by fitting plane shapes together without gaps.

Tessellation comes from the Latin word *tessella*, which was the name for a small piece of coloured stone used by the Romans to make mosaics.

Tetrahedron

A tetrahedron is a polyhedron with four triangular faces.

A regular tetrahedron has an equilateral triangle for each face.

► equilateral triangle, polyhedron, pyramid

Thousandth

1. Thousandth (1000th) is the ordinal number of a thousand.

The thousandth person to visit the website was given a prize.

► ordinal number, tenth

2. A thousandth is the fraction $\frac{1}{1000}$.

A metre is a thousandth of a kilometre.

Three-dimensional (3D)

A polyhedron is three-dimensional because it has length, breadth and height.

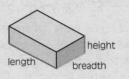
height
length
breadth

► breadth, height, length, two-dimensional

Time

Time is an occasion or period measured in seconds, minutes and hours.

The actual time varies around the world. When it is midday in London it is 7:00 a.m. in New York.

► analogue clock, calendar, digital clock

Times (×)

Times is a way of saying 'groups of' or 'lots of' in a multiplication fact.

3 times 8 is 3 lots of 8 (8 + 8 + 8), which is 24.

► multiply

Ton

A ton is a measure of mass or weight in the imperial system. A ton is 2240 pounds and weighs a little more than a tonne in the metric system.

A large car weighs about 1 ton.

▶ imperial system, ounce, pound, stone, tonne

Tonne

A tonne is a measure of mass or weight in the metric system. A tonne is 1000 kilograms (kg) and weighs a little less than a ton in the imperial system.

10 large adults would weigh about 1 tonne.

▶ gram, kilogram, metric system, ton

Torus

A torus is a solid ring shape with a hole in the middle.

Total

The total is the result when you add together a group of numbers.

The total of 6, 7 and 8 is 21.

$6 + 7 + 8 = 21$

▶ addition, sum

Transformation

A transformation is a change made to the position and/or size of a shape.

Reflection, rotation and translation are all transformations.

▶ reflection, rotation, translation

Translation

A translation is a movement of a shape in a straight line. Every point of a shape that is translated moves the same distance and direction.

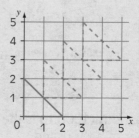

The shape has moved up and to the right.

▶ transformation

Trapezium

KS2

A trapezium is a polygon with four sides. Two sides are parallel and two sides are not. A trapezium can have two right angles.

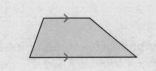

▶ polygon, quadrilateral, trapezoid

Trapezoid

KS2

A trapezoid is a polygon with four sides. It has no parallel sides and can have one right angle.

In the USA the trapezium and the trapezoid are the opposite shapes to those in the UK, so their trapezoid has two parallel sides.

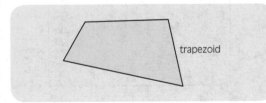

trapezoid

▶ polygon, quadrilateral, trapezium

Travel graph

KS2

A travel graph is a line diagram showing a journey, in which distance is plotted against time.

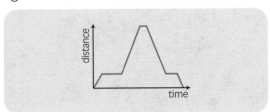

Tree diagram

KS1

A tree diagram has branching, connecting lines and is used to show decisions or results in a diagram form.

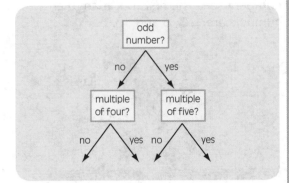

Trial and improvement

KS2 ????

Trial and improvement is a way of looking for a solution to a problem by putting in a guessed-at value and looking at the results. This can be done several times, each time getting nearer and nearer to the correct answer.

Trial and improvement can be used to work out the length of sides of a cube with a volume of 100 cm³.

Triangle

KS1

A triangle is a 3-sided polygon. The three angles of a triangle always add up to 180°.

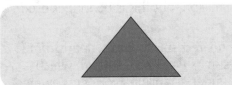

▶ equilateral triangle, isosceles triangle, polygon, right-angled triangle, scalene triangle

A B C D E F G H I J K L M N O P Q R S T U V W X Y Z

Triangular number

KS2 1234

A triangular number can be arranged as a group of dots in the shape of a triangle. The number of dots is the same as the number itself. The first four triangular numbers are 1, 3, 6 and 10.

6 is a triangular number.

▶ square number

Triangular prism

KS2 ○△□

A triangular prism is a prism with a cross-section of a triangle.

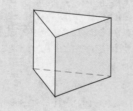

▶ cross-section, prism

Trillion

KS2 1234

A trillion is one million million, written as 1 000 000 000 000.

In the UK, a trillion used to be 1 million million million, but this is no longer used.

The nearest star to Earth, apart from the sun, is Proxima Centauri, which is just under 40 trillion kilometres away!

▶ billion, million

Triple

KS2 +−×÷

1. To triple is to multiply by 3.

Triple 3 is 9.

▶ double, quadruple

2. The number that is three times another number is a triple.

9 is the triple of 3.

▶ double, quadruple

Two-dimensional (2D)

KS1 ○△□

A polygon is two-dimensional because it has length and width but no height (thickness).

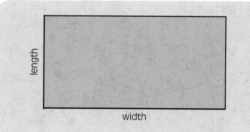

▶ breadth, length, three-dimensional, width

Unit

1. A unit means one: a single thing or a single number.

> 1 unit of electricity costs 6.5 pence.

2. A unit of measurement is a standard amount of that measurement.

> A metre is a unit of measurement equal to 100 cm.

▶ kilogram, litre, measurement, metre, second

Unitary method

The unitary method is a method used in problems which involve calculating the value of one item and multiplying by the number of items required.

> Sam pays £8.50 for 5 pens. How much will he pay for 3 pens? A single pen costs £1.70 (£8.50 ÷ 5) so 3 pens cost 3 × £1.70 which is £5.10.

▶ multiply

Unit fraction

A unit fraction has a numerator of 1 and any number as the denominator.

> $\frac{1}{2}$, $\frac{1}{7}$, $\frac{1}{25}$ are all unit fractions.

▶ denominator, fraction, numerator, proper fraction

V

KS2 1234

V is the symbol which stands for 5 in the Roman numeral system.

VIII stands for the number 8.

► C, D, I, L, M, Roman numerals, X

Venn diagram

KS1

A Venn diagram is a way of showing how different things can be sorted into groups. The groups are known as sets.

Venn diagrams are named after the mathematician John Venn (1834–1923).

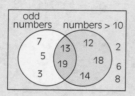

► Carroll diagram, set, sort

Vertex (plural: vertices)

KS1

A vertex is a point where two or more lines meet to make an angle. It is one of the corners of a triangle, square or any polygon or polyhedron.

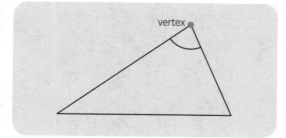

vertex

► corner

Vertical

KS1

1. Vertical means at right angles to the horizontal.

2. A vertical line is at right angles to a horizontal line.

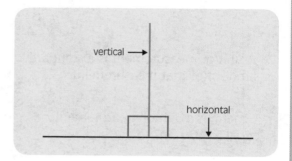

vertical
horizontal

► horizontal, right angle

Volume

KS1

The volume of an object is the amount of space it fills. It is measured in cubic centimetres (cm^3) and cubic metres (m^3). To find the volume you multiply the length by the breadth by the height. It is sometimes written as: $l \times b \times h$.

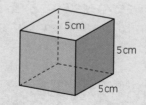

5 cm

The volume of this cube is
5 cm × 5 cm × 5 cm = 125 cm^3.

► capacity

Vulgar fraction

► common fraction

86

Week

A week is a period of seven days. A year has 52 weeks and one day (or two days in a leap year).

Monday, Tuesday, Wednesday, Thursday, Friday, Saturday and Sunday are the names of the days of the week.

▶ day, hour, month, second, year

Weigh

You weigh something to find out how heavy it is.

The bag of sugar weighed 1 kg.

Weight

Weight is the heaviness of an object or person. The force of gravity pulls objects down and gives them weight. We usually measure weight in kilograms (kg) which are really units for measuring mass.

My friend is the same weight as me. We are both 58 kg.

▶ mass

West

West is one of the four main points of the compass, opposite to east and 90° anticlockwise from north.

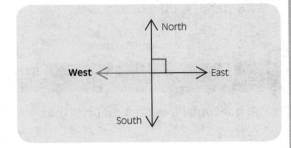

▶ compass, east, north, south

Whole number

'Whole numbers' is a loose term and can mean both natural numbers (1, 2, 3 etc.), or integers, so they can be positive or negative numbers. They have no parts that are fractions and they can include zero.

The whole numbers between 3 and 7 are 4, 5 and 6.

▶ integer, natural number

Width

Width is another name for breadth. It is a measure of how wide something is – the distance across from one side to the other.

The width of this river is 45 metres.

▶ breadth, length

X

KS2
1234

X is the symbol which stands for 10 in the Roman numeral system.

> XX stands for the number 20.

▶ C, D, I, L, M, Roman numerals, V

x-axis

KS2

The horizontal axis on a graph is the *x*-axis.

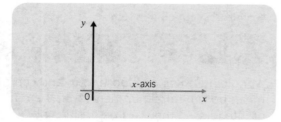

▶ axis, *y*-axis

Yard
KS2

A yard is a measure of length in the imperial system. There are three feet in one yard.

> 1 yard is approximately equal to 1 metre and is about the length of a long stride made by an adult.

▶ foot, imperial system, inch, metre

y-axis
KS2

The vertical axis on a graph is the y-axis.

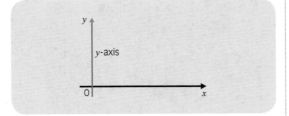

▶ axis, x-axis

Year
KS1

A year is the period of time it takes for the Earth to go round the sun, approximately 365 days.

> A calendar year has 12 months.

▶ calendar, day, leap year, month, week

Zero (0)
KS1 1234

Zero is the symbol for nothing or nought. It is written as 0. Zero is neither positive or negative and in our place value system it is used as a place holder.

> Three plus zero equals three.
> Three minus zero equals three.
> Three multiplied by zero equals zero.
> Three divided by zero equals infinity.

▶ place holder